CORRECT IDEAS
DON'T FALL
FROM THE SKIES

CORRECT IDEAS DON'T FALL FROM THE SKIES

ELEMENTS FOR AN INDUCTIVE THEOLOGY

Georges Casalis

Translated from the French by
Sister Jeanne Marie Lyons
and Michael John

ORBIS BOOKS
Maryknoll, New York 10545

The Catholic Foreign Mission Society of America (Maryknoll) recruits and trains people for overseas missionary service. Through Orbis Books Maryknoll aims to foster the international dialogue that is essential to mission. The books published, however, reflect the opinions of their authors and are not meant to represent the official position of the society.

Originally published as *Les idées justes ne tombent pas du ciel*, copyright © 1977 by Les Editions du Cerf, 29, bd Latour-Maubourg, Paris

English translation copyright © 1984 by Orbis Books, Maryknoll, NY 10545
Bible quotations are from the *Jerusalem Bible*.

Library of Congress Cataloging in Publication Data

Casalis, Georges.
 Correct ideas don't fall from the skies.

 Translation of: Les idées justes ne tombent pas du ciel.
 Includes bibliographical references.
 1. Theology. I. Title
BR118.C2413   1984   230   83-19374
ISBN 0-88344-023-7 (pbk.)

*To my friend Maurício López,
peaceful militant and courageous witness,
philosopher and theologian,
rector of the University of St. Louis,
professor at Mendoza and Buenos Aires,
taken from his home January 1, 1977,
by a group of armed and masked men—
and since then . . .?*

Where do correct ideas come from?
Do they fall from the skies? No.
Are they innate in the mind? No.
They come from social practice
and from it alone. . . .
—Mao Tse-tung, 1963

Contents

ix

Preface

Each of the following chapters is complete in itself. Readers may wish to read them in some other order. They might want to search for the starting point of an approach that moves from practice to interpretation, from experience to the clarification of certain theoretical principles, from life to an attempt to grasp its meaning. The position taken here is that all theology should follow this route. The essential difference comes from militancy and the options that it implies. Perhaps chapter 6 will provide the key to all the reflections initiated here. And after all, why not, even if the decisions that have given a completely new orientation to my life as a theologian were made much earlier? The orientation of this book is indeed based on the attention I have given to the intellectual and spiritual crisis of our times, which reflects the deep malaise to be found within the various pieces of a shattered Christianity.

In any event, militant groups will find in these pages a certain number of indispensable points to be included on their agenda: awareness of the roles and functions of the dominant theology, rediscovery and rereading of the scriptures, reshaping the requisite dimensions of hermeneutics, reformulation of one's identity in relation to Jesus of Nazareth, a political reading of daily happenings and personal life, and critical institutional practice.

Unwillingness to face up to the considerable difficulties presented by each of these points could well mean turning away from the gospel. In any case, nobody is going to develop a taste for these questions by evading them but by plunging deeply into them or, rather, by letting them penetrate deeply into oneself.

It should prove no surprise to find a number of quotations,

some of them lengthy, included as part of the text. Their presence is less to draw attention to obvious relationships than to emphasize essential solidarities and, even more than that, to provide a hearing for those to whom I have listened for a long time before beginning to speak.

Preface to the English Translation

The reader will notice that events in Cuba and Vietnam have played a decisive role in forming the awareness that has given rise to this book. The German, Spanish, and Italian translations of it were published when Vietnam was being hard struck by the Chinese invasion, coming in the wake of natural catastrophes (floods and droughts with serious consequences for the rice harvest) that had already rendered the situation dramatic—to say nothing of the cessation of American aid in the south of the country and of Chinese aid in the north. This heroic people is learning tragically that it is more difficult to win peace than war. The misery it had succeeded in keeping at bay for thirty years of resisting successive waves of invaders came back in force, with all its physical and moral consequences.

And as if this was not enough, a forceful propaganda campaign has tried to discredit Vietnam by claiming that its government has created a real "Gulag Archipelago" in Southeast Asia, ruled by political terror and repression. What a stroke of luck for the bourgeois press and its fanatical anticommunism! Sincere journalists and political figures have been seen suddenly to lose their balance and join in the most formal denunciations. I have closely examined the general statements and the statistical details that have been handed out, and have collected all the firsthand information I could get from Vietnamese friends, especially from their courageous Christian communities, as well as from well-informed persons who have recently visited there. All of them declare that, despite the harsh conditions resulting from real problems, and the only too real aftereffects and threats of war, there is no reason to burden Vietnam with suspicions as unwarranted as they are clearly motivated by self-interest. As usual, to seek the origin of this campaign is to discover its malicious intentions and the political effects that were expected of it, both on the international level and on that of popular struggles in diverse countries throughout the world.

So I declare here that I continue to profess friendship and admiration, trust, and solidarity, with the Vietnamese people. Without in any way idealizing its regime or political methods, I refuse to see in Vietnam a failure of socialism, as all those who are troubled by the present advance, the world over, of the forces of revolution would be happy to believe.

Introduction

This work is the fruit of a long journey, a journey made as an individual and as a member of a community. I should like it to be true to scientific methodology but not to the point of being abstract and "impartial." Why? Because the method used is related to an end, which is liberation. It is—and will be taken, therefore, as—subversive.

It has long been admitted that it is impossible to be neutral with regard to politics. Like any other discipline, theology cannot be neutral; the more it claims to be, the less it actually is. In the work at hand, then, I have chosen to be partisan and to say so frankly at the start. The only objectivity to which I lay claim is the objectivity of being committed, of being a militant. Perhaps this admission will lead some readers to close the book at this point.

A personal consideration will help to situate the context of these reflections that have now reached a certain stage of development. They are provisional and imperfect but nonetheless decisive, having crossed a threshold that admits of no return. Among a number of other occasions, three dates have marked awakenings in my life that have had consequences I am still unable to fathom.

On January 30, 1933, Hitler seized power in Germany. On that day, as I have often been aware since, I became an adult, politically speaking. I understood that I was enlisting in resistance, and that my whole life would be a struggle for my fellow human beings—against everything that threatens them, against all the absolute idolatries that claim definitive control over their fate, against the cold and anonymous monsters that arrogate exorbitant rights to themselves—in defiance of the fact that a government has only duties to fulfill for the collectivity, whose servant it is.

Clandestinity and illegality did not come to an end in 1944. It is

1

a curious experience to learn that they will always hold an important place in the life of anyone who will never accept giving in to the strong arguments of power, whatever label or form it may have. And if certain leftist friends of mine accuse me of being an impenitent anarchist and of not knowing that there is a time for an ethic of conviction and a time for an ethic of responsibility, I am resolved to persevere in unconditionally refusing to accept the intolerable, wherever it is to be found and in whatever guise it may appear. No authority can be rightly established and justly exercised that does not agree—or want—to be challenged *from within* by the very ones who most desired its coming and contributed most to its final realization.

The prophets could not be deterred from their vocation. For them justice was always an end above and beyond winning and exercising power, even when this is done by close comrades. As far as I am concerned, I have neither the health nor the competence for a political career. Besides, I have chosen another profession, that of a theologian, and I am completely happy to be able to practice it. My position is that the democratic control of power—and that includes reminding those in power to pursue its true ends—is the responsibility of every citizen. Rightly understood, this is the way for those at the grass roots to express their prophetic role.

On November 23, 1946, in the midst of negotiations for peace with Ho Chi Minh and possibly by the unilateral decision of a French admiral, Haiphong was bombarded. In a few hours we were responsible for between six and twenty thousand deaths. We were into our first colonial war after the liberation of France. If not at that moment then at least shortly afterward, I understood that it was not enough to have "driven the enemy out of France" to be free, but that it meant we had to be resolved never to oppress anyone. The saying of Marx—extended to include every possible dimension—became one of the central themes and driving forces of my life: Any person, any party, any class that oppresses another cannot be free. It was easy to have a good conscience during the occupation, when we were completely dominated by an inhuman foreign power and were fighting against it. But when we ourselves, having barely escaped from the "Thousand-Year Reich," behaved, on an international and interpersonal level, as if we were Nazis dealing with Jews and Poles, how could we continue to talk about national honor, how could we look ourselves in the face? To confront the horror of Haiphong as well as the extortions perpetrated in Germany after the French Army crossed the Rhine and, above all, the widespread atrocities done in Algeria, has been the hardest conceivable schooling in humiliation for a French resistance fighter like myself. The most distressing realities challenge us, accuse us. We have no other response than Dietrich Bonhoeffer's: Loving our country means being able to fight it in order to defeat the oppressive rule that it exercises over others.

The third date will not be recorded in world history. It was in December 1957. I was at the Ouchaia Wadi, a horrible shantytown in Algeria where men, women, and children were subsisting in an indescribable subhuman state. Suddenly, in a particularly filthy hut where I was helping distribute flour, I was overcome by an irresistible wave of class hatred. It was an experience all the more disturbing because, until that time, nothing had prepared me for it. The liberation of the area and the colonial fight for independence appealed to other motives. Here the evidence was overpowering—nothing at all could justify such misery, which was the direct result, the legitimate offspring of our conquest and occupation of that country. I can still hear one of my companions muttering, "After a hundred and thirty years of French presence. . . ." And I know that at that moment I would have been capable of any kind of "terrorist" act, no matter what, against a system that had not only tolerated but engendered the slow and violent death of "underdeveloped" multitudes. Yet at the same time I knew that my class hatred was self-hatred, hatred of myself as a beneficiary and an accomplice of the colonial system as well as a product and an exported expression of the capitalist order. Middle-class persons who undergo such an experience, if they do not make their escape through the distractions at their disposal, cannot help hating themselves. Surely it is not by chance that the Gospel of St. Luke, the gospel of the poor, speaks of *hating* one's family and one's life as the first condition for becoming a disciple of Jesus (Luke 14:25–26).

There are only two solutions: suicide or conversion. Conversion itself is a form of death, a severance from a previous way of life, rebirth into a struggle for the present and future of humankind. Since that day at Ouchaia, I have experienced elsewhere an unexpected surge of the deep hatred that energizes the never ending protest of the masses—in Algeria, in shantytowns, in France, in the outskirts of Vientiane where newborn babies were disposed of on the dung heap, in the infernal immensity of Netzahualcoyotl in Mexico, where a million and a half human beings stagnate with no reasonable hope of any change. After a day spent in that ocean of dust, one of my Jesuit friends, an animator (against all hope!) of a production cooperative, asked me, "What have you to say about it?" I exploded, "There are only two solutions—an atomic bomb or the resurrection of the dead!" Later on, in Cuba, in Hanoi, I saw that something else—revolution—can put an end to unmitigated misery.

The present work originated as an expression of this conviction and the practice it has occasioned. Let me reassure you; I have no intention of giving an account of what I have been doing by way of practical implementation. All the same, I know that it is upon practice that I can be judged—and by anybody—on condition that those who judge submit themselves to the same criterion, and provided that their judgment serve as an occasion for resurrection and love.

Readers should understand that it would be difficult for me to adhere strictly to a dispassionate methodology from beginning to end. This work is not going to be devoid of emotion; passion will be part of it, giving it spirit and life. Would a dispassionate theological work reflect the activity, the life, and the death of Jesus of Nazareth? However, there is no indulging in mere passion: an attempt to be clear-sighted is behind each stage of development.

An undertaking of this kind runs the risk of oversimplification. The need for brevity can only increase the probability of succumbing to that risk. I shall, therefore, begin by making three important clarifications.

1. In this book, when reference is made to the "dominant theology" (the ideology of domination), my intention is to gather into one single convenient concept the diverse institutional and mental structures that characterize the traditional Christianity of the majority of Christians. These represent differences that are,

however, less profound than they appear to be. In spite of a number of contradictions that can be pointed out, and to which we shall return later, the use of the term "dominant theology" is not arbitrary. It serves to identify a certain consolidation of ideas, the kind of consolidation observed in 1971 after the Protestant Federation published the document "L'Eglise et les pouvoirs" ("Church and Powers"). This resulted unexpectedly in the creation of a united front against it, an odd, heterogeneous assemblage of theologians and lay persons of all denominations who, until then, had sincerely believed that they were opposed to one another on essential matters, their confessions of faith. They proved to be at one in their categorical rejection of the document. Their credos seemed suddenly to have become less important, like superstructures on a common base, a reality that they had all chosen as a class and were not at all prepared to question.[1]

2. The term "revolution" also requires some clarification, although those who know full well what it sets out to do would prefer not to hear about it. It should be said that we cannot have *the* revolution but only some concrete revolutions located in time and space in response to the people's will to put an end to iniquitous regimes of institutional violence. Every authentic revolution aims to accomplish three objectives that relate to the three levels of capitalist domination—exploitation, oppression, and alienation:

a. The appropriation by the collectivity of the means of production and distribution as a first condition for an *economic* revolution and the establishment of elementary justice.

b. The establishment and continual renewal of the forms of popular power—that is, of the *political* constitution of society—not tolerating power *over* and power *for* the people—even if it is the power of a workers' party—for the inception of an organization that would provide for the exercise of power *by* the people. The term "grassroots control" symbolizes what is at stake: the guaranteed personal and collective freedom without which every revolution ceases to advance and becomes corrupt.

c. The liberation of creativity, "imagination come to power," the generation of new lifestyles, new kinds of activities and celebrations, new ways of interpreting the meaning of life, a transformation of relationships between cultures and individuals, the search for personal happiness in a setting that offers equal opportunity to all—everything characterizing an *ideological* development consonant with changing economic and political structures.

As the people of Cuba, Vietnam, and Mozambique have discovered, an authentic revolution aims at the emergence (collective and individual) of a *new human being*. This means that there is a risk involved, that something is at stake, that the pursuit of revolution never reaches an end, and that any attempt to pin it down is to stifle it (see Appendix, IV, p. 191).

3. The perspective of this book is West European. There is where I have my oldest, if not my deepest, roots; this is where I am bound to participate in the struggles for the future. If I were living in a socialist country, the confrontations would be quite different. But I shall take care not to conduct such confrontations on behalf of anyone else. It is a matter of taking action in the place where I am. In choosing such a context, let us opt for the concrete. The risks, sufferings, and progress made by others cannot substitute for asking our own questions and for finding our own answers.

European capitalism in crisis can offer nothing but dead ends to the people of Europe and the rest of the world. The system has no solution to put forward. The only hope lies in revolution, in *breaking out* of a system based on more and more structural violence and evolving toward greater and greater injustice. There is no question of finding within it something to imitate, some model. All that matters is the goal to be reached. What in other places is achieved through elections, or by nonviolent action, armed guerrilla warfare, or other forms of activity, open or clandestine, must here be achieved by the most appropriate means to be found.

The object of this text is not to debate about revolutionary militancy but to reflect on its spiritual consequences. How to engage in it is not all that clear. On the other hand, when it asserts itself, it plainly demands that every "value" justify itself. What is of moment for the dominant theology—the ideology of domination—is that the dominated are challenging "the established disorder" (Mounier). That is the object of our present reflection.

"Elements of an inductive theology" is an ambiguous and hardly satisfactory expression; yet it offers the advantage of clearly indicating opposition to the deductive approach of traditional theology. Instead of setting out from a "revealed given," it begins with actual experience. Who in the world could begin anywhere else? To use a popular image, do not the laborer and the philosopher have to sit on the same bench? Reflection, together with a reading of the gospel related to militancy—both of them secondary to involvement—is the approach here. As a consequence, few *a priori* definitions have been given. As we move along, those that are needed will be developed.

Among the factors that have contributed to the maturation of what is expressed in these pages, interdisciplinary research done by the Ecumenical Institute for the Development of Peoples[2] and the Protestant Institute of Theology has played a decisive role. Various writings and, in particular, the records of sessions held on religion and liberation under the chairmanship of Pablo Richard have provided indispensable material to complete this study.

Chapter 1

Flowers among the Ruins

Blind Alleys and Unmarked Paths

Look at theology today as the twentieth century is coming to a close and what do you see? Ruins. It is up to us not to celebrate and still less to mourn the sight but to try to understand what lies before us. First of all, we need to define our task. Today we are presented with an enormous literary output in the fields of scripture studies, history, and sociology. Christianity is under investigation—its basic texts, its actualizations in history, the impressions that it has left with us and the characteristics it has today, the influence that it still exercises on individual minds and group mentalities—all this is scrutinized, analyzed, and measured with more and more refined and less and less arbitrary scientific methods. Teams of researchers, unhampered by any concern for apologetics, are doing their rigorous and exemplary utmost to achieve an indispensable and impossible objectivity. Today anyone who wants to become informed about the origins of Christianity as well as its past and present reality has at hand instruments, documents, statistics, and evaluations unavailable twenty-five years ago.

Yet all of this is only the antechamber to theology. Something more than a mastery of all the methods of research is needed to cross its threshold. Nor does being an ultrazealous pamphleteer get you in. Our times have proved fertile in producing partisan libelers. They play by no rules, engage in confused brawls, and throw religious rocks in every direction. Theirs is the very contradiction of the scholarship backed up by laboratories and learning centers.

These libelers begin by setting to work on the names for God, which are often only ciphers for the self-divinization of the combatants; they square off, leap for each other, grapple, and embrace—the better to throttle one another. As one critic said after a television match between two Dominican antagonists, the only loser was the one true God . . . if God exists. Of course, theology is of necessity polemical, but it should not be blind, and it must not serve as the locus for settling accounts or as an alibi for engaging in confrontations stemming from other sources. Even granting that pamphleteers may be honest and sensitive, they generally lack the sound scientific temper indispensable for theologians, an objectivity analogous to the attitude scientists have about the impact of their basic research on reality.

Theology should be a methodological endeavor and a prophetic testimony, leaving aside both the charismatic anarchy of the pamphleteer and the aloofness of the scholar. It should have roots in the soil of Christianity and in the earth of daily life; it should lay bare the underground bases and conditionings of evangelical life and throw light on its never ending search for meaning today; it should take care to foster a twofold credibility grounded in a creative continuity of tradition and in a type of life and presence that speaks with eloquence. If fruits are an unimpeachable proof of the stock that bears them, why should they not continue to mature on the parent tree? In his own way, a biblical author was saying the same thing at the end of the first century: "Jesus Christ is the same today as he was yesterday and as he will be forever" (Heb. 13:8).

At the present time, theology has retreated in the face of an impossible task and the risks involved in it; there are almost as many Christian martyrs in the world today as there were during the entire history of the early church. Theology as I have described it has become a rare commodity in our contemporary world, particularly in any systematic form. To achieve the kind of synthesis characteristic of the discipline from the days of Augustine of Hippo to Karl Barth is impossible now; it can only present us with an image of Christianity itself; it is a splintered mirror. In countries of great theological traditions, such as those of Western Europe, it is hard to name even two or three renowned theologians capable of creating theological systems—that is, of being innovators of original and timely syntheses for the service of Catholic, Orthodox, and Protestant communities. The great majority do nothing but dust off and re-present what others have already said, or they confine themselves to peripheral matters. Linguistics, although its importance is central, often offers the opportunity to avoid the risk of speaking a new word for the age. The key debate in Germany—concerning the scientific status of theology—provides a cover to hide the sterility obtaining in a country that for a long time provided a model for others in the same field.

There are exceptions, of course, at once happy and minor; minor because, after a season of greatness, we have now attained the average; happy, because a living theology is being born, and born elsewhere and otherwise than in the past. It is more often engendered in communitarian experiences than in the silence and isolation of academic chambers, and in different and less weighty forms than professional productions.

Walter Benjamin writes:

> Today we turn to facts rather than to convictions on which to build our lives, to facts that have as yet never become a basis for conviction anywhere in the world. Under these conditions engagement in literary work cannot be successful if carried out exclusively in a literary milieu—the classic expression of sterility. Authors can accomplish meaningful literary work when they alternate between doing and writing. New forms—whether tracts, brochures, reviews, or posters—more suitable for exerting influence in the arena of action rather than in the universally accepted realm of books, must be created. Only fast-paced communications can respond to the need for action at the present time.[1]

What Benjamin singles out is characteristic of the new theological style and the reason why, among the ruins of university productions and far away from hallowed halls and developed countries, some small flowers of unknown and fascinating forms and scents are appearing here and there. Grafts have been made, seeds have been sown to the winds by many demonstrations—of workers, peasants, and students—by freedom movements in Vietnam, Mozambique, and elsewhere. Their significance for theology is obvious. We shall be coming back to this later.

Stages of the Dominant Theology

Here I should like to take time to review a brief analysis of the history of theology presented by Bishop J. A. T. Robinson in his *The New Reformation*, who cites one of his Catholic colleagues who shortly after "went wrong"—obviously by getting married—and so had to find new surroundings[2] in which to continue living as a theologian.

Bishop Robinson writes:

For a point of departure I would turn this time to a Roman Catholic. In a recent article in *The Downside Review* Charles Davis wrote illuminatingly of what he called "the ecology of theology."[3] By this he means the influence of the environment on theology in different periods and situations in the church's life. He traces, so far, four different theological "cultures" in the history of Christendom:

1. "Theology in the patristic age," he says, "was predominantly an *episcopal* theology. The leading theologians, such as Athanasius, Basil, Augustine, were bishops; and even where theological works were not written by bishops, they are strongly marked by the pastoral concern of the Church." And he sees this type of theology, like all the others, as one of abiding necessity for the life of the Church. "There is a contribution to theology that can be made only by bishop-theologians. The fact that no bishop, however theologically minded, would bother with some of the questions discussed by theologians would have a purifying effect

on theology were bishops more closely involved in theological activity than they are.''

But the distinctive characteristic of this type of theology, as each of the others, is not primarily *who* does it or *where*, but the thrust and motive-power for it. In this first instance theology is a function of *episcope* or oversight, of feeding, guiding and ruling the flock. It is the kind of theology which a bishop is charged at his consecration to guard and guarantee. But it is certainly not the exclusive prerogative of bishops. Indeed, most of the historic names in the Church's theology fall naturally into this category—not only Athanasius and Augustine, but Luther and Calvin, Hooker and Wesley, Forsyth and Barth. In the Church of England it has traditionally been pursued, not only or even chiefly in episcopal palaces, but in cathedral closes and country vicarages; and its latest example of such a theology of episcopal care and oversight is the work of a layman, the report of Mr. Leslie Paul on *The Deployment and Payment of the Clergy*. In all our traditions today the most characteristic manifestation of this type of theology is to be seen in the official commissions appointed by a denomination or Council of Churches.

2. The second milieu of Christian theology was the *monastic*. Indeed, in eastern Christendom this has always been its most creative environment. Theology here is a function of contemplation, and its motive power is supplied by needs of the ascetic and mystical life. But, as Mr. Davis notes, it has also a strong literary element. It corresponds, indeed, within the Christian Church to the movement that flowered in the wisdom literature and the scribal tradition of Judaism.

3. The third characteristic form of Christian theology was the *scholastic*, taking its distinctive color from its university setting. Here the dominant drive has been the assimilation and communicating of learning for its own sake. This type of theology has been one of the great glories of Western Christendom. It has been the fount of pure scholarship without which the stream of theology soon becomes muddied and stagnant. Whatever the pejorative associations of

the word "academic," it is clear that no living church can afford to neglect its discipline or allow its decline.

4. Finally, in his thumbnail sketch of theological ecology Mr. Davis notes the dominance of what he calls *"seminary theology,"* since the Reformation. Indeed, in his own communion post-Tridentine theology has been almost entirely shut up in the seminary, especially in a country like England. Its motive power has been the training of a professional clergy, and increasingly in all our traditions over the last hundred years the seminary has been the seed-bed (and often also the hothouse) of our theological culture. No one would deny the pervasive contribution made to the life of the Church by this tradition of teaching and study. It is the theology not of the bishop or the monk or the professor but of the pastoral counsellor, and without whose competent contribution in recent decades the Church would be in a sorry way.[4] Nevertheless, "theology in seminary confinement," as Mr. Davis entitles his article, has disturbing features, especially when pursued in isolation.

But my concern is not to examine these, as he does, but to ask whether in the twentieth century we are not being challenged to yet a fifth theological type. It is certainly not to be seen as an alternative to the other four as if they were mutually exclusive. Nevertheless, if we fail to develop it and remain content with the theologies shaped by the creative forces of other situations, we may default disastrously on the task ahead of us.

For want of a better term, I will call this fifth type a *lay* theology. By that, of course, I do not mean an amateur as opposed to a professional theology. Nor do I mean a theology for the laity in the narrow sense of those who are not clergymen, though one would expect its distinctive character to be moulded by laymen, in the same way as the typical practitioners of episcopal theology have been those charged with *episcope* in the Church of God. In its essence it is a theology impelled by the needs of the *laos,* or whole people of God, to *be* the Church *in* the world. Just as in the past it has been the councils of the Church, the monasteries, the universities, the training seminaries, that have been the springs from which new theological thinking has been fed into the Church, so tomorrow I would hope its creative source to be the engagement of the *laos* in the life of the world.

The organs through which this theological thinking will most distinctively be done have yet to be fashioned. But the embryonic forms of them are doubtless visible in the lay institutes, the evangelical academies, the ecumenical centres, and, in much humbler but no less important ways, the listening-posts of Christian presence and Christian dialogue in a predominantly post-religious world. . . .

This . . . means nothing less than an institutional revolution for the Church. It means taking with absolute seriousness "the servanthood of the laity" in the world "not as a nice addition to round off a professional ministry but as *the* ministry of the church."[5]

This notable presentation of the history of theology serves as a good beginning for us. It has the advantage of not indulging in caricature or disparagement. There is no question of denigrating or condemning the first four stages of theological production. They responded to many of the legitimate needs of the life of the church in the past and had a certain number of common characteristics:

1. They were loci of *knowledge* and *power* because the theology that they produced was the primary ideological instrument in the service of church government. This is true even of the theology that was rooted in monastic life and developed as a reaction to the savorless doctrine taught and the slack morality incarnated by the secular clergy. Its purpose was to bring the whole church back to its original purity and to total fidelity to the gospel. The learning elaborated and taught during the four stages—or cultures—had as its end the continued existence of the ecclesiastical society that gave it birth. Professional theologians with outstanding expertise and rhetoric in matters of religion were called upon to lead and defend the Christian flock against heresy and any kind of deviation. (And often they acted with the sort of energy exerted and the means employed by Dominican inquisitors and by Calvin too in the trial and condemnation of Servetus!)

Although the Reformation made grand assertions about the priesthood of all the baptized, Friedrich Daniel Schleiermacher, the father of contemporary Protestant theology, could write at the dawn of the nineteenth century that the aim of theological education was to produce "virtuosos of religion," who would also be the "princes of the church" for modern times. A little later, Alexandre Vinet, the French-speaking theoretician of Protestant pastoral theology, described the pastor as the Christian par excellence, a model for the community, a brilliant and heroic captain equipped to lead Christ's troops into battle.[6]

2. As a matter of fact, the alliance of theological knowledge and ecclesiastical power does create a group of Christian elite ordained, of course, for the service of the whole church but set apart and above ordinary Christians as lesser folk. These become dependents and minors who, if they are to outgrow that state, must do so through the mediation of those whose learning appears sanctified by ordination. Even when claims are made to the contrary, the baptized are subordinated to theologians, priests, and pastors, and subject to their authority in doctrinal, disciplinary, and ritual matters. In the most anti-Roman Protestantism, the pastor becomes and remains the president of the council of elders, the speaker charged with explaining and applying scripture, the one who knows biblical languages, the experienced exegete who, on the authority of the Bible and in God's name, pronounces on what is correct doctrine and upright conduct.

The feeling of inferiority is so deeply ingrained in the laity that, if by chance any of them attain some leadership positions in the church, they make haste to attach themselves to some professional theologians who become their permanent consultants, indispensable references, and the real voices of their consciences.

3. The importance of the clerical power structure has not gone unnoticed by those with political power, and they have done everything to harness and tame it. Recall the role of the emperors at the time of the ecumenical councils during the era of episcopal theology; the protection accorded by princes and kings to the monasteries charged with education and, consequently, with the formation of a people; the utilization of medieval universities by the feudal system and of seminaries by the bourgeoisie. All are too obvious to require any lengthy disquisition. The numerous

exceptions represented by many saintly bishops, monks, theologians, and martyr-pastors count for little compared with the interminable litany of theoreticians of Caesaropapism, the part-monk and part-colonizers, the missionaries of white dominant civilization to "primitive" peoples, and the religious agents of the C.I.A. operating today throughout the world under the most diverse confessional labels.[7]

Theo-ideology

The dominant theology, whatever its hue, is imposed in this way because it is, in very fact, a theology of domination, produced by religious power structures in the service of the dominant classes of developed societies—that is, of societies organized to maximize their power and wealth by means of the economic exploitation and ideological conditioning of the dominated masses within the rich nations and in the countries of the Third World—or the "Two-Thirds World," according to another way of viewing it.

Without developing the Marxian analysis in "The German Ideology," I include it here:

> In every epoch the ideas of the ruling class are the ruling ideas, that is, the class that is the ruling *material* power of society is at the same time its ruling *intellectual* power. . . . The ruling ideas are nothing more than the ideal expression of the dominant material relationships grasped as ideas; that make one class the ruling one and therefore the ideas of its domination.[8]

Traditional theology, whatever its nuances may be, or rather whatever its internal contradictions may be, is the religious component or aspect of dominant ideas.

The closing years of our century are seeing a radicalization of anticapitalist and anti-imperialist class struggles. Where feudal, colonial, and multinational empires are being brought down or strongly contested by oppressed peoples in their struggles for freedom, there is a real proportion between what is happening to them and the devastation taking place in dominant theologies, accompanied by the emergence of other—popular and revolutionary—readings of the gospel.

The famous "Christian identity crisis," talked about so much and with such distress, could well be linked to the challenging of national and international powers by the human masses that are becoming quickly and increasingly conscious of themselves, of their true identity, and are expressing it in their rejection of the exploitation, domination, and alienation they have suffered for centuries because of the economic, political, and religious powers of "Christian nations."

If an illustration of what has been said is needed, the following extract will serve. It is taken from the *Chilam Balam de Chumayel,* a Mexican Amerindian composition of the seventeenth century:

Mourn their coming,
the sad day of their coming.
Alas for Itza, the wizard of waters.
Our gods count for nothing now.
The true God who comes from the sky
speaks only of sin, teaches only of sin.
Inhuman are his soldiers,
Fierce and cruel his hounds.
Only because of the folly of the times,
Only because of the folly of the priests,
unhappiness came upon us.
Those exemplary Christians came with their true God,
and it was the beginning of our unhappiness;
the beginning of misery,
the beginning of tribute,
the beginning of almsgiving,
the beginning of covert discord,
the beginning of battles with firearms,
the beginning of clashes,
the beginning of pillage,
the beginning of debt enslavement,
the beginning of debt that cleaved to the skin,
the beginning of continual quarreling,
the beginning of suffering.

It was the beginning of the work of the Spaniards
   and the religious clergy,
the beginning of the practices of tyrants,
   of schoolmasters and catechists.
Even children, little children,
were martyred!
Unhappy the poor
who went into slavery without protest,
into slavery to the anti-Christ on earth,
to the tiger terrifying the people,
to the panthers terrifying the people,
to the vampire terrifying the poor Indians.
But the day is coming
when the tears of the people
will reach up to the throne of God
and the justice of God will come down
like lightning
on the world.
Surely it is the will of God that Ah-Kantenal and Ix-
   Pucoyal[9]
return to strike them from the face of the earth.[10]

This is only one example, from among millions, of a non-Christian countertheology. And it is quite clear that no argument based on the religious domination exercised by the priests and leaders of "primitive" peoples could justify the continuance or restoration of a "Christian" order. On a worldwide compass, and whatever the "benefits" and "correctives" that the church has generally employed to offset the excesses of economists, politicians, and military experts, the role of the productive structures of the dominant theology has been largely negative. By breaking with those structures, peoples and their leaders have found or rediscovered themselves and plunged into struggle, working out Christian countertheological formulations along the lines of those studied here.

We should not think that we are dealing with something existing only in faraway places such as Latin America and southern Africa; the conflicts among the Irish and among the people of Jura, Switzerland, where Protestantism plays the role of the dominant theology, and among the Lebanese, where Catholicism is in the service of repression, provide examples of close-to-home situations where these analyses apply. It is important to emphasize that in these three cases, contrary to a simplistic interpretation of Marx, the religious dimension has served to radicalize conflicts between classes and make them apparently insoluble. If some class conflict is the basis of historical confrontation, then when class barriers coalesce with religious divisions, a sort of metaphysical venom pervades the antagonism. When the awakening of the oppressed occurs in a religious framework contrary to their oppressors', it should not surprise anybody if ecumenism, traditionally considered to be apolitical, is also blown sky-high.

The dominated and marginated peoples coming into their own is a phenomenon that is close at hand and is obviously urgent and important. As Michel Clévenot writes:

> Today we ourselves are conscious of belonging to minority, marginated groups. The struggles that we are carrying on against religious ideology and its (re)productive mechanisms make two demands of us: (a) We must learn the conditions in which an ideology, especially a religious ideology, is reproduced. This requires a historical (diachronic) as well as a systematic (synchronic) study. (b) We must replant our roots in the more or less underground currents that, over two thousand years, have brought us the dynamisms to which the Bible bears witness, and that are still moving us today.
>
> In sum, what we have to do is find the means for reshaping a memory of militancy. Our tendency is to leave history too much to specialists (just as we do with the Bible) on the pretext that the pressing demands of the present absorb all our attention.[11]

"The People of God" (?)

Returning to the fifth source of theological production envisioned by Charles Davis and quoted by J.A.T. Robinson, a careful critique will of necessity come to denounce the ambiguity of the notion of a "people of God" as applied to the church and used

to define the "lay" character of the theology of the new reformation. To be sure, in the recent history of Catholicism and, in particular, in the texts of the Second Vatican Council, especially *Lu-
men Gentium*, this expression has played an increasingly
significant role in accentuating the importance of the priesthood
of the baptized in relation to the ministerial priesthood and has,
consequently, proved a challenge to clerical monopoly. Yet, at
the same time, the particularist character of the church in relation
to the whole of humanity, its depiction as a community of a
higher quality and with a special responsibility toward non-
Christians, has not been discarded. Even if the distinction between clergy and laity has been attenuated, the distance between
Christians and other human beings has not been lessened.

What is called for is the unity, the collective solidarity, needed
by those who belong to different spiritual and ideological families
in view of a future that all will share. To distinguish between those
who are "of God" and those whose qualifications to be so called
are not patent to us is, in fact, highly questionable. Does not such
discrimination contain the seeds of new religious racisms and all
the political baggage that they imply? And does not the post-
Vatican II "broadened particularism" go counter to the sweeping
world vision of the biblical authors? As someone has written,
"The Church of Vatican II wants to serve but is not ready to be
poor."[12]

A few remarks will suffice here:

1. In the key text of Exodus 19:5, a "people of God" has a
separate existence (as a part of the whole!) only to show that *the
whole world belongs to God*. The Jewish people is to be a testimony to this, not by conquest or colonization, but through the
revelation of a spiritual dimension common to all human beings.

2. In the New Testament, each time the church is designated as
the "people of God," it is by analogy with the Jewish people and,
therefore, as a reminder that its basic nature is not to be a ghetto
but a structure open to all comers.

3. Other passages of the New Testament accentuate this dimension, in particular Acts 18:10 in speaking of "the many" belonging to God in Corinth—that is, of the whole population in which
the Christian community represented only a very small minority.
Texts of Revelation—5:9; 7:9; 10:11; 14:16—reflect a recapitu-

lary view of the whole human race finally brought together in a new unity transcending all the conflicts of history. In 21:3 this consummation appears as a gathering of all peoples around the living God in the new city: "Here God lives among men. He will make *his home among them; they shall be his people,* and he will be their God; his name is *God-with-them.* "

4. It can be stated without hesitation that the New Testament is unacquainted with a people of God apart from others; it knows it as a fundamentally relational community ordered to all humankind, a sign of hope that the gospel will shine on all peoples, a "new creation" (2 Cor. 5:17; Gal. 6:15), a new humankind—that is, of all of humanity reconciled and united in peace and justice (Eph. 2:14 ff.; 4:7-13). Early Christian writers made this their central interest. The church has meaning and reality only as an instrument of eschatological unity. Everything that particularizes the church by putting distance between it and world history and, even more, by assigning it an end in itself, diverts it from its vocation and robs it of meaning.

This brief survey of biblical theology—approaching it very much in the classic mode and not at all "inductively"—suggests a critical rereading of the Davis-Robinson passage and points up the surprisingly narrow limits of the most progressive traditional theologies. Here are some points I should like to make about it:

1. Robinson does not break with the elitist thinking of church authority circles when dealing with the question of lay leaders, of well prepared lay persons. Furthermore, these persons themselves continue to be marked by centuries of clerical domination. Often quite creative and innovative in the "profane" (professional) aspect of their lives, they frequently manifest astonishingly childish reactions about their spiritual life and their participation in church activity. Even "frontline" bishops are surprised to encounter resistance and "ideological backwardness" when even the best of their flocks are faced with taking concrete initiatives in pastoral and liturgical renewal. Basically, inside every Christian is a dormant Lefebvre, a silent singer hymning in secret the old negro spiritual, "Give me that old-time religion."[13] Nevertheless, conservative Christians are a contradiction of the black slave who sang nostalgically of an exodus to a land of promise, because what conservatives want is to be secure in a well-padded world

where religion is unchanging and they are safeguarded against the risks of modern times.

2. Classic theology, even when progressive, simply moves the barrier forward but leaves it intact. Robinson makes the interesting proposal of "starting from the other end,"[14] with "a truly lay theology,"[15] "a theology impelled by the needs of the *laos,* or whole people of God."[16]

During the feudal period, bishops, monks, and theologians were in charge of the laity; in the day of liberal democracies (is it still with us?), the bourgeoisie of the church has assumed the task and marked off the general lines along which the laity's being-in-the-world is to be defined. This surely means taking up in a sympathetic and critically helpful way the lost gamble of the Reformation: that the people as a community be responsible for witnessing to the gospel. However, because to do that persons have to be able to read and write and organize, the members of the bourgeoisie are the ones who appropriate power and exercise it: over the right, by limiting institutional conservatism; over the left, by restraining the revolutionary impulses of the masses. The absence of the masses from and indifference to the "great" churches demonstrate how futile is the effort to define a theology in this way. Just as the bishops, monks, and professors used to function, so leading members of the laity do now. They are *of* the laity, they want to be and are *for* the laity, but they are not *with* the laity. They, too, govern, serve, and domesticate the laity; they do not want the laity to become free. As a Catholic militant vehemently expressed it, " 'They' have not accepted the fact that a member of the laity is not of their mind. 'They' have not grasped the fact that lay persons work and have to earn their living. 'They' want the laity to comply with things they themselves do not observe!"

3. Only the elimination of this barrier and the abandonment of a certain way of thinking make sense and can lead to a popular theology. Contrary to popular religion, which voices both the alienation of the masses from the dominant theology and their protest against it, a popular theology is consonant with adult awareness and liberating practice. The biblical view sketched above shows clearly that a distinction between the peoples and *the* people is made only with a view to the unity of all. The liberation

of all humankind is the primary task that all of those who belong
to the Christian community must share. A new theology will arise
only when the needs *of the people*, of the human multitudes, and
especially of the poor and the oppressed, have been realistically
addressed.
These needs are really responded to only when a people converts them into the driving force for the achievement of realistic
utopias. A popular theology cannot, in any case, be a reflection of
any sort of paternalistic solicitude of prominent lay persons
stooping down to be helpful to others. It must be the awakening
of a collective consciousness for combat, for commitment to
bring about a new society and a new humankind. If Christians
participate in the struggle exactly as others, without special privileges or protection, without remaining aloof or seeking an escape,
and if they go on to a rereading of the gospel as the very heart of a
common militancy, then will the flowers of a popular theology
spring up among the ruins of all the great religious systems of
domination.
Such readiness is to be found in the well-known pastoral letter
of Bishop Huyghes of Arras written in March 1972 on the occasion of a visit by the French prime minister, M. J. Chaban-
Delmas, following demonstrations by workers:

> Christians, both workers and officials, joined their com-
> rades in the legitimate defense of their employment, which
> is increasingly under fire in the region. These Christians
> were the church, and they did not wait for me to make it
> present. Silence is imposed on the poor of the world, on the
> poor of Pas-de-Calais, in the name of economic necessity or
> of political prudence. But if the poor are silenced, Chris-
> tians are entitled to provide them with a voice.[17]

Militancy and Theology

Robinson saw the problem when he wrote:

> The new Reformation . . . has not only a revolution in the
> theology of the laity to see through. It has, I believe, the still
> more far-reaching task of moving towards a genuinely lay

theology—which may indeed prove the distinctive contribution of our period to the history of the church.[18]

Everything depends on the expression "a genuinely lay theology," which is analogous to Bonhoeffer's intuitions about "a nonreligious Christianity." In his case, it had to do with Christianity lived in the perilous situation of being engaged in a plot to overthrow Hitler—that is to say, a spirituality for a dangerous involvement with a form of oppression. "A genuinely lay theology" would therefore have its origins in the life of the people and in militant participation in the people's struggles for liberation. In cases where militancy does not wipe out the faith but, on the contrary, purifies and renews it, then a popular theology, in the service of a future popular church, begins to germinate.

What is happening not only in Latin America but in Vietnam and Algeria as well, where a very interesting Islamic socialist hermeneutic is in the process of formation, shows without a doubt that this is not a left-leaning intellectual fancy.

Whoever speaks for militancy must speak for an enlightened partisan option. If the popular masses, animated by their most alert and alive elements, are making history, it is because they are moving in a definite direction: the destruction of systems of oppression and exploitation, whatever they may be; the acquisition of power by the people; the attainment not only of a sufficient level of material well-being but, more than that, of coresponsibility, creativity, dignity, and happiness. This utopia, denounced by all pessimistic sin-oriented theologies and by all religious prophets of doom, must give life to a methodological optimism that is a secular version of eschatological hope, and it must be held onto in the face of daily reverses and failures. Joining Teilhard de Chardin in saying that we must be integrated in a "common front of all who believe that the universe is still evolving and that they have the duty to help it evolve" is not enough.[19] Militancy names the enemy forces—not just to denounce them but to analyze their power and to develop an apt method to defeat them. Understanding the enemy forces, defining strategic objectives and tactical means, organizing concerted action to take the successive steps to revolutionary victory is praxis. Praxis breaks away from abstract and general discourse; it is concrete, firmly situated in space and time; it conforms to the lines adopted by class struggles. Becoming a militant means being identified with class struggles.

We come back to the lines that prompted these reflections: "Where do correct ideas come from? . . . the skies? No . . . they come from social practice." It has nothing to do with working out a theoretical definition of a new type of theology; it means working at praxis and, very precisely, at revolutionary praxis, the primary prerequisite for the elaboration of a popular theology. Later on, we may look at the pros and cons for the acceptability, the necessity, of such an elaboration. For the present, to indicate that it is possible is all that is intended. The "inductive" approach consists in rereading the gospel and Christian tradition by beginning with praxis—that is, by concrete practice in the conflicts between classes. Let me emphasize it once more: should what is being said here remain at the level of discourse, it would be one of the worst embodiments of the idealism characteristic of theologies of domination. And all too many contemporary experiences prove that, because of the "ideological backwardness" earlier referred to, the ruptures that must be made often get no further than words and have no relationship to an effective practice of class struggle. Some theologians think that they have recovered, through fresh discourse, a virginity long since besmirched by continued prostitutions with the dominant classes. They are wasting their time. The oppressed recognize at a glance their true allies and their real enemies.

Praxis is the primary and categorical prerequisite for a popular theology. It would be well for us all to be wary of employing this formula as a weapon against anybody as long as we have not resolved to face up to ourselves every day and to use it for measuring our own acts of cowardice and betrayal when we encounter the demands of the struggle. Nothing could be worse than to have a new sect put in an appearance among the ranks of contemporary Christianity—a sect of pharisees dedicated to talking about praxis. The provocative cynicism of Marcel Lefebvre is to be preferred; he at least has the asset of single-mindedness and shows clearly his practical solidarity with politicians of the right and the extreme right. We should all then apply to ourselves the hard and sound gospel saying, ". . . you will be able to tell them by their fruits" (Matt. 7:20). Non-Christians, sickened by the contradictions of religious idealism, apply the same rule to Christians.

A closing remark may be useful here. Those who declare themselves and show themselves to be partisan will hear on all sides from cautious thinkers who detect in their behavior the malaise of persons of good families who have become ashamed of their origins and their education. And they will say that persons always remain what they are, that they cannot shed their own skins. What curious representatives they are of a gospel that has much to say about *metanoia*—of repentance, or better, of conversion, a move that is not only a break with the past but also with structures guilty of crimes against humanity. It presupposes a commitment to a future of justice, solidarity, and liberation. Luke's John the Baptist has some unmistakable things to say along this line.

Marxists are less unbelieving than are many church members. Rightly thinking that every person is first of all a social being, they do not blame others for having been born and (de)formed in a particular social group, for being the historical products of the economic and ideological conditioning of their class. They call this their *class situation*. On the other hand, and contrary to the supporters of bourgeois religion, who obviously reveal in this way the kind of gods they worship, Marxists in no way consider conditioning by origin and culture as a natural given, a destiny. They know from experience that it happens often and everywhere that persons become conscious of the criminal character of the system maintained by the class to which they belong, that they break with it and engage in revolutionary praxis. The choice of a class replaces submission to a class; this is a *class position*, and this is all that counts. The masses have always accepted into their ranks members of the bourgeoisie who have made a definitive break with their class situation. These include Ernesto "Che" Guevara and Marx, who made the bold statement, "As philosophy finds its *material* weapon in the proletariat, so the proletariat finds its *spiritual* weapon in philosophy."[20]

Fidel Castro had the same thing in mind when he told the Chilean Christians for Socialism, "I say without hesitation: We see in

Christians of the left, in revolutionary Christians, strategic allies of the revolution.''[21] Anyone who knows how to distinguish between tactic and strategy could not underestimate the extraordinary implications of this statement for the future of a whole continent—at the very least.

Chapter 2

The Writing of History

The Impatience of the Poor

The relationship between profession, social status, practice, faith, and theology appears definitive not only for the "inductive" approach that I have quite consciously adopted—and about which I must express myself as fully and accurately as possible— but for *all* theology as well. The dominant theology, with all its claims to be universal and perennial, is also rooted in distinct historical and social practices and structures: those identified with the domination of European peoples by politico-religious classes and castes and, through an extension of that domination, of the peoples of other continents by colonial and missionary activity. In these areas, as in the homelands, theology has generally served to hallow and justify the established order, at times criticizing its excesses but not taking issue with its very principles and doing nothing to contest the founding and building of colonial empires. On the contrary, it has conferred on them the absolute character of divine law.

Among numerous examples, the instance of Vietnam can be cited. In 1928 the constitution of the Evangelical Church of French Indochina referred to chapter 13 of the Epistle to the Romans as a scriptural argument to support an article stipulating that "anyone opposing the government cannot be admitted into the Evangelical Church of French Indochina." This was expressed in such clear detail that no one could fail to grasp what it meant:

28

The Evangelical Church of French Indochina declares that it remains ever loyal to the established government and never permits its adherents to rise up in any way against the authorities. As for itself, it never becomes involved in political matters [sic] or with anything foreign to the spiritual end that is its constant pursuit, as the present statutes clearly show.[1]

In 1951, the Catholic bishops under the direction of the Irish Vicar Apostolic John Dooley, appointed after Msgr. Drapier had been recalled at the request of General de Lattre de Tassigny, issued a pastoral letter decreeing the incompatibility of patriotic activity—participation in the freedom struggle under Ho Chi Minh's leadership—and membership in the Catholic communion:

Joint Letter of the Ordinaries Meeting at Hanoi

The bishops of Vietnam, moved by the confusion existing in the popular mind, believe it to be their duty to define clearly the idea of homeland. Patriotism is love of one's homeland, and homeland [French *patrie*] is, etymologically, the land of our forefathers. Homeland is, then, an extension of the family; the virtue of piety has to do with both, and, consequently, we can only encourage and develop it just as we do other Christian virtues. The Christian idea of homeland does not exclude other nations, which we should love as well because we are all children of the same God.

Animated by our feeling of grave responsibility before God and by a great affection for all of you, our very dear compatriots, we judge it to be our duty to put you on your guard against the grave danger of atheistic communism, the greatest danger of our times. Communism denies God, denies all religion, denies the existence of an immortal soul, denies the rights of the human person and of the family. Such complete opposition exists between the Catholic Church and communism that our Holy Father has proclaimed that it is absolutely impossible to be a Catholic and a communist at the same time, and that any Catholic who belongs to the Communist Party is by that very fact separated from the church. Not only are you forbidden to belong to the Communist Party but you cannot cooperate with it or do anything whatsoever that could help in any way to bring it into power. The danger is so grave and the possible consequences so terrible that we feel obliged to put you on guard as well against the diversionary tactics and stratagems used by the communists to deceive the people, tricks that serve nothing but the ends of communism.

In the first place, they make a great show of zeal for social reforms and put forth their doctrine as a remedy for the social ills of our day. They conceal themselves under a mask of patriotism and, by their pretense of zeal for the well-being of their compatriots, they seek to rally others to their banner. This is simply a means to attain their secret ends. Once in power, they establish a ruthless dictatorship. Then the interests of the poor, of the workers, give way to the interests of communism. Thus, in countries under the yoke of communism, private ownership is suppressed and thousands of Catholics suffer persecution. They live in terror, waste away in prisons, and even pay with their blood for their fidelity to the faith.

And so, most dear brothers and sisters, resist, do not allow yourselves to be deceived, be faithful to your God. Be vigilant, be strong, remain firm in the faith. And you, dear priests, teach the social doctrine of the church, instruct the people in the Christian virtues of charity and justice. Priests and faithful, live your Christian lives wholeheartedly, following the precepts of the gospel. The charity of the early Christians led to the conversion of the world. Charity means befriending our neighbors, forgiving them, wishing them well, and really doing good to them. The love of God has overcome hatred; your charity will overcome the hatred of the enemies of God. Let your life be always a witness for God, for Christ, and for the church.

In conclusion, together with St. Paul, we say to you again, "Be awake to all the dangers; stay firm in the faith; be brave and be strong. Let everything you do be done in love" (1 Cor. 16:13-14). We ask our priests to read this letter in all churches and chapels. To all, priests and faithful,

we give our paternal blessing with a full heart. May the grace
and peace of God our Father and of our Lord Jesus Christ
be with you.

John Dooley
Vicar Apostolic of Indochina

Hanoi
November 9, 1951

Added were the signatures of the bishops and vicars apostolic
of Nam Vang, Vinh Long, Saigon, Qui Nhon, Hung Hoa, Phat
Diem, Hue, Bui Chu, Bac Ninh, Hanoi-Haiphong, Thai Binh,
Kontum.[2]

In both these cases, one Protestant and one Catholic, the dominant theology and discipline are put completely at the service of
the colonial order—to bring about submission to it. More than
that, the churches did not hesitate to organize Christian militia,
which distinguished themselves by appalling horrors at the time
of the "pacification" of the Red River delta. A summary of the
socio-political expression of this theology was given by Pope Paul
VI in a classic formula to the Colombian crowds gathered at
Medellín; in substance, it asked the poor to be "patient" and the
rich to be "generous." As if the rich ever gave up their privileges
except when the impatient poor forced them to do it!

In 1974, the Dutch Reformed Church of South Africa showed
no reluctance in making the following collective pronouncement:

A political system based on the development of the particular characters of diverse ethnic groups can be fundamentally
defended in the light of the gospel. Nevertheless, the commandment of love of neighbor must be maintained as the
ethical norm for a just regulation of relationships between
ethnic groups.[3]

So, once a basis for the system of apartheid has been established in scripture, love is going to reign among ethnic groups.
Other Christians will denounce such a position, say that it is a
monstrous heresy and that, moreover, the church that professes it
has broken with the World Council of Churches. No doubt, but is
it so different to preach love in a society where no questions are

raised about capitalist class structures? It is ironical to talk about love and reconciliation while making no move, either on the practical or the theoretical level, against structures of injustice guaranteed by institutional violence.

"The Bandung of Theology" (Yves M. Congar)

The impatience of the poor is bringing about the downfall and disintegration of the dominant theology. This became evident with the historic conference on church and society that took place at Geneva in 1966; with the emergence of Latin American theologies of liberation beginning in 1968; with the Bangkok conference on evangelization at the end of 1972 and, in the same year, with the appearance of Christians for Socialism in Chile; and finally, and especially, with the "Final Statement" of the Ecumenical Dialogue of Third World Theologians at Dar es Salaam in August 1976.

As spokespersons for the poor of the Third World, this group provided us with a mirror reflecting the pillage and murder committed by the "developed" countries and echoed the cry of the impatient poor calling the dominant theology to account. The still striking remnants of that theology may provide us with some majestic ruins, but they can no longer conceal the fact that they are essentially an expression of the cultural privileges of the ruling classes of the northern hemisphere; they have no objective correspondence with faith and practice among the exploited masses in the Third World or in countries called "developed."

On this subject, the Dar es Salaam statement is inexorably clear. After tracing the history of the origins of the Christian missions and paying tribute to the zeal and devotion of the missionary founders of the "young churches," it has the following to say:

19. All the same the missionaries could not avoid the historical ambiguities of their situation. Oftentimes and in most countries they went hand in hand with the colonizers—both traders and soldiers. Hence they could not but be, at least partially, tainted by the designs of the searchers for

gold, spices, lands, slaves, and colonies. While they were zealous for souls, *they tended to think that the commercial and military expansion of Western peoples was a providential opportunity for the salvation of souls and the spread of the evangelical message.*[4] Thus they collaborated in the colonial enterprise, even when their Christian consciences sometimes felt revolted by the atrocities of the brutal colonizing process. Hence it is necessary to distinguish their good will and the substance of the Christian gospel from the actual impact of the Christian missions in these countries.

20. The missionaries could think of the spread of Christianity in terms of transplanting the institutions of their Euro-American churches within, of course, the framework of imperial domination. *Thus the new Christians were segregated from their fellow human beings* and alienated from their traditional religious and cultural heritage and their community way of life. This process strengthened their hold on the new believers. The liturgy was imported wholesale from the "mother churches"; so were the ecclesiastical structures and theologies. *A pietistic and legalistic spirituality* common in Europe at the time was introduced into the new churches also. In later times, the Western educational system was instituted in the colonized countries largely through the services of the churches. We have thus the establishment of Christian churches in these continents more or less as carbon copies of European Christianity, adapted, however, to the subject situation of the colonized.

21. In the early phases of Western expansion the churches were allies in the colonization process. They spread under the aegis of colonial powers; they benefited from the expansion of empire. In return they rendered a special service to Western imperialism by legitimizing it and accustoming their new adherents to accept *compensatory expectations* of an eternal reward for terrestrial misfortunes including colonial exploitation. The crafty merchants and soldiers of the West were not slow to see and take advantage of the presence of missionaries among their captive peoples. *The gospel was thus used as an agency for a softening of national*

resistance to plunder by the foreigners and a domestication of the minds and cultures of the dominated converts. In fact, the foreign powers often gave the Christians a privileged position of confidence within their arrangements for the administration of the countries. In the process Christian teaching got badly tainted by the search for selfish gain of the peoples who called themselves Christian and exercised power in the name of emperors and spiritual rulers.

22. The theology of the Christian churches at this time not only suited the colonization process but was also fed by it. The sense of military and commercial superiority of the European peoples was underpinned with the view that Christianity was superior to other religions, which had to be replaced by "the truth." *For centuries theology did not seriously contest the plunder of continents and even the extermination of whole peoples and civilizations.* The meaning of the message of Jesus Christ was so blunted as not to be sensitive to the agony of whole races. These are not merely sad historical realities, but the immediate antecedents of contemporary Western theologies. *For these latter have not yet learned to contest the successors of the colonizers—viz., the powerful countries of Europe, North America, and Japan. Nor have they evolved a theology to counteract the abuses of the heirs of the colonial merchants, viz., the giant predatory multinational corporations of today.*

23. The Christian churches in the tri-continental colonial situation fostered educational and social sciences that helped improve living conditions for the population of these countries. Unfortunately their value patterns were such as to fit into the capitalistic domination and hence were largely academic and individualistic, with the result that the leadership to whom independence was granted in the colonies (except after a revolutionary struggle) were generally persons schooled in the Western capitalistic tradition. *In this way the churches—perhaps unwittingly—contributed to the formation of the local elites that were to be the subsequent collaborators in the on-going exploitation of the masses of the people even after political independence.* The social services

too, while relieving immediate needs, failed to generate a critical social conscience or support the radical movements for social justice. The churches thus generally continued to be a sort of ideological ally of the local middle classes that joined the power elite and shared economic privileges with the foreign companies that continued even after political independence (in Latin America from the nineteenth century and in Asia and Africa after the mid-1940s).

24. We see in the churches in the three continents the growth of a "liberal" trend in more recent decades, as a successor to the traditional "conservative" position. The liberal trends are in favor of the adaptation of the churches to the indigenous cultures and to the operation of parliamentary democracy within the framework of free enterprise capitalism. Local religious, priests, and bishops have replaced the foreign ones. The theology was thus adapted to suit the postindependent situation. *However, there was not yet a fundamental alliance of the churches with the masses struggling for radical social justice.*[5]

Apparently, every theology is linked with class practice and so its nature depends upon the character of the class with which it is linked. Yet the difference between a "deductive" and an "inductive" theology is, in reality, secondary to the decisive discovery that neutrality is impossible, and that anyone who does not side with the oppressed is, in fact, whether consciously or not, an accomplice of oppressors. At the very most, the dominant theology can be credited with believing itself to be deductive, universal, and perennial while unconsciously playing the part of "an inductive theology of domination." But is being unconscious a valid excuse in a matter that calls for clearheadedness as a primary and unfailing requisite?

Theologians of the Third World stress that for them the criteria for the credibility of European theologians consist in their breaking away from structures of domination, their standing up to the powerful countries of Europe, North America, and Japan, their counteracting the abuses done by the heirs of the colonial merchants—the multinational corporations, the great plunderers of today. In a word, Third World theologians judge the evangelical authenticity of their European colleagues by their political praxis.

The Inductive Approach of All Theology

The "inductive" nature of deductive theology—that is, its ideological character in the negative sense of the term[6]—is beginning to be uncovered by theologians formed in the best schools but later at odds with them. Jean-Marie Aubert, professor on the faculty of Catholic theology at Strasbourg, is a case in point. Under the title "Political Components of All Theological Reflection," he has presented an elucidation of how theology has, throughout history, taken on an ideological character related to the environment in which it was formed. He notes that some historians have called the first great ecumenical councils "imperial parliaments," because they were the only assemblies that gave counsel to the emperors, but at the same time, they were totally conditioned and largely controlled by them. This opens our eyes to the effective relationship between the conditions in which the great dogmas formed after the fourth century were elaborated and their role in the political life of the Roman empire. He shows how power took over theology, and how the process of osmosis operated between the ideology of the established order and theology:

> The title "Son of God, Savior" is a classic appellation for the emperor. In use especially from the time of Augustus to the time of Constantine, *Theou huios soter*, was later applied to Christ. The analogies between imperial pagan theology and Christian theology cannot be interpreted as a real dependence of the latter on the former; nevertheless, there has been, along with verbal transference, a conceptual transmission, which should not be underestimated and which indicates a political component within the very notion of salvation, so intimately a part of Christian faith.[7]

This means that the emperor is not the Son of God, but does it not result in Christ being put in the place of the emperor? The imperial image of Christ that is thus introduced into history will later serve as an alibi for all the Crusades and attempts to colonize so-called pagan territories. Catholic kings will shamelessly organize one of the greatest crimes of Christian history: the genocide of the American Indians, which is still going on today. In other words, to take the emperor's title and apply it to Christ is indeed an affirmation that Caesar is not God, but is it not at the same time a way to make Christ look like a Caesar? That is not political or ideological innocence.

Another delightful passage of Aubert concerns St. Thomas and medieval theology:

> As an example of such juridical integration in matters where one would least expect it, let me mention the angelic hierarchy. What role does scripture attribute to the nine categories of angels that it enumerates? Beginning with the classic idea that angels are ministers of God, St. Thomas makes the nine categories correspond to the political functionaries of the Middle Ages, most of whom bore titles borrowed from Roman law.

And again:

> If the old theocratic dream has evanesced with the formation of nations and the emancipation of temporal power, it has at least survived in the idea that the church has developed of itself as an institution, an idea that lives on in our times, even if we have somewhat forgotten its political components: a monarchical, authoritative, vertical, pyramidal conception of ecclesial power. (In time, the clergy was to become one of the three estates in the society of the *Ancien Régime*.)[8]

Interestingly, even non-Roman, very small religious communities have a nostalgia for the unitary medieval system. Aubert says that "no theology can be judged in advance as untainted by any political infiltration."

We see, then, that theology, like every other human undertaking, is a political undertaking, and becomes, very possibly without any intention or consciousness on the part of those theologizing, a reflection of the established order. It serves, as a matter of fact, to maintain that order. This happens because of naivety vis-à-vis the environment in which theology is formed. Theology is a component of the ideology that supports the existing order.

Numerous examples could be given. To mention a case in point, most translations of the Bible say that Barabbas was a "brigand." To qualify Barabbas as a brigand puts him into a moral category: he is an evil blackguard, and Jesus is really good to take the place of an evildoer. The trouble with this picture is that, by going a little more deeply into the Greek text, we ascertain that the term *lestes*, which designates Barabbas, is a term having as its first definition "a member of a fighting band" of zealots, or fedayeen—in a word, a guerrilla! So Barabbas moves from a moral into a *political* category. And it becomes apparent that it is not the same thing to say that the death of an innocent man gives freedom to an evildoer, or that the death of a nonviolent man gives a fanatical nationalist a future. This shows how much an ideology can influence translations of the Bible.

Harvey Cox has emphasized how striking it is that sin is generally spoken of in the category of revolt (against God). Why? Because the established order has a vested interest in branding revolt (against the powers that be!) as sinful. And this in spite of a whole series of biblical texts denouncing as sinful the evasion of responsibility for history, failure in human solidarity, and the refusal to stand up for the rights of the poor.[9]

By giving sin an individualistic character, a vertical dimension, and a metaphysical coloring, we reduce the collectivity to atoms. We all stand alone before God, preoccupied with the purification of our own souls. If we are unaware that sinning against God is always, to begin with, wronging a brother or a sister, if we fail to recognize that, in the first place, it has to have a horizontal dimension and a socio-historical bearing, are we not running the risk of one day having the people rise up to demand justice and to reject every sacred dimension in their lives because the political dimension has gone unrectified? Are we not to take seriously the message of Amos, who denounced every liturgy carried out in a social context in which the poor are exploited? If "true worship" means the establishment of a more human society that adumbrates the heavenly city in history, then it is very evident what a work of upheaval noble hearts are called upon to perform in their progress toward sanctity and their search for inner peace. Does not the denunciation of "red priests" arise from among those who keep telling themselves that the priest's business is with the gospel alone, and who claim never to have anything to do with politics and forbid the church to commit itself in that arena?

Prominence is given to certain theological themes that do not take issue with the value systems of the established order. That involves nothing Machiavellian: the linkage between the dominating power and the ideology of domination is so natural, unchanging, and subtle that even those who want to denounce it become blind and deaf to the most elementary and obvious gospel realities. Oscar Cullmann has pointed out that, in Constantinian society, the title most frequently attributed to Jesus, the title of "servant," received no elaboration in Christology, whereas the title of "Lord" had the evolution with which we are familiar. It was preferable for the emperor, the earthly lieutenant of a glorified Christ, to have for his "patron" a heavenly king rather than a slave in the service of love.[10]

Abbé Pierre once exclaimed that the worst thing about the rich is that they are dumb brutes, incapable of knowing what real life is and the actual lot of the human beings around them; they are completely possessed by what they *have*; they have lost the possibility of *being*.[11] True, no doubt, but their dullness does not exclude a redoubtable sharpness in defending their interests, in acquiring additional privileges, and in consolidating their power.

Only another and different social practice makes a rupture with establishment theology possible. And this new practice will find an ally in another type of theology, not, as Latin Americans insist, just another theme for traditional theology but *another theology*, voicing clear situational and existential options. An "inductive" approach is indispensable. But it should be quite evident that the would-be deductive method is not the vice that disqualifies traditional theologies. What nullifies the traditional theologies is, above all, *the part they play in serving the ruling classes*. Napoleon Bonaparte, an expert in this area, put the case with luminous precision:

> As far as I am concerned, what I see in religion is not the mystery of the incarnation but a mystery of the social order: it prevents the rich from being massacred by the poor by relegating the idea of equality to heaven.
>
> Religion is also a sort of inoculation or vaccine which, while satisfying our love for the marvelous, protects us from charlatans and sorcerers; priests are worth more than Kant[12] and all the German dreamers put together.
>
> Without religion, how could we have order in the state? Society cannot continue to exist without inequities in personal fortunes; for inequities to continue we must have religion. When someone is dying of hunger and someone else nearby has everything, it would be impossible for the starving man to acquiesce to such a disparity if there were no authority to tell him: God wills it so; in this world there must be rich and poor but in the hereafter for all eternity, fortunes will be reversed.[13]

When we think of the tremendous imprint that Napoleon I left upon the whole world—and upon religious life in France—we can only wish that we could find among contemporary theologians the clarity of mind possessed by the cynical man who inspired the civil code, the Concordat of 1801, and the articles of law still in force in Alsace and Moselle. Those who would like to see in religion only the mystery of the incarnation would do well to give their attention to the relationship it could have to the social order. The way ideologies have permeated traditional theologies points the way for them.

At all events, the inductive character of all theology seems obvious; no Christian discourse exists that is not rooted in a substratum of positive or negative class practice, and that does not reveal the situation as well as the position of the person articulating it. Robinson is right to question the social roles of those who formed traditional theology. (It would also be reasonable to inquire into the lifestyles and standards and the material exigencies of certain theologians.) In any case, it is unquestionable that being "lay" and being "militant" are not the same.

What Are Scriptural Texts?

We have reached a point where it is important to clarify the nature of the scriptural texts that have always served as a departure for deductive theological approaches. These are going to have an entirely different but no less decisive status in the praxis of militant Christians.

The German theologian Gerhard von Rad, a specialist in Old Testament studies, defines Israel's credo as having three articles: election, exodus, conquest—three events linked with three men, Abraham, Moses, and Joshua;[14] three moments of history decoded and translated in relation to one another as three actions accomplished by a people who afterward said, "They were given to me by the One who rules over history." The credo of the church is not fundamentally different as to its origin. As Kant well observed, it is a value judgment based on an experience of Jesus, on coming in contact with Jesus. Then what happens?

A man, Jesus of Nazareth, enters history, and meets other human beings; he lives with them and they live with him, and at some moment those persons make a value judgment, "That man is the Christ." Curiously, it was always others who said it of Jesus. He did not say it of himself, and refused to claim messiahship, affirming it only when it led to his condemnation to death.

We believe on the basis of what we have lived, we believe *a posteriori* according to our life experience. All scriptural texts are about circumstances, all about incidents. Not a single text of deductive theology is to be found in scripture; that includes the prologue of the fourth gospel, which elaborates an experience, "We saw his glory" (John 1:14), and the texts concerning the Eucharist (for example, 1 Cor. 10 and 11) that St. Paul composed because there was a crisis over the eucharistic celebration in the church of Corinth. It was in regard to that crisis that the apostle said: "Let us be careful and remember what the Lord has instituted."

The inductive approach is indeed as constitutive a part of the scriptural texts as it is, in general, of ideological products. No text is independent of the economic and political conditions in which it first saw the light of day; nor is it free of the class conflicts of the milieu in which it arose. Saying this—does it need to be spelled out?—is not in any way denying "divine intervention" or what is called "inspiration." On the contrary, it means taking the incarnation seriously, accepting the fact that the Word, the self-witness that God imparts in the human witness that Jesus gives to God, is expressed and transmitted in every era by social beings to other social beings. In no way does this mean that someone touched by the Word is kept from being a person of responsibility, committed to being "a person for others."

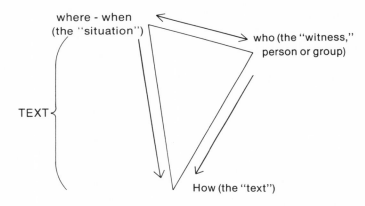

Diagram 1

Every scriptural text can be thought of as a triangle in which three elements meet: the "who," the "where-when," and the "how"(Diagram 1).

The "who" is the witness, the historical agent who "reads what he or she sees."

The "when-where" is the situation.

The "how" is the literary form, the text the written word used by the witness to communicate a message, something that seems of importance at the time. Dynamic relationships of fruitful tension exist between the witness (the bearer of a message who is aware that he or she is neither its author nor its owner but has received it from elsewhere) and the situation, which conditions the author and which the author strives not only to explain but also and particularly to transform. The writing, the "how," is the result of the encounter, often of a conflictual kind, between the situation and the witness. The situation has geographic, historical, socio-political, and cultural (Semitic) characteristics; it conditions, without absolutely determining, the witness, who represents a situation, a class status, social mores, but also—how could it be otherwise?—a temperament, a spirituality, a style of life and writing.

To understand a text, we must not only decode, translate, and analyze what is written but also reconstruct the situation and the role that the witness played in it. (The introductions and notes generously provided in recent editions of the Bible make a useful contribution to this end.)

Because of this very fact, the written word cannot be identified with the Word, which is to be found somewhere within the dynamics of this relationship of triangular tension. Nothing is more misguided than the integralist or fundamentalist attitude that attempts to find "the Word" in the written word alone, whereas any word is alive only if it is not fixed, if it implies and creates a relationship to both synchronic and diachronic time, time experienced in one far-reaching moment and time experienced as historical, as lived out by successive generations. To reduce the text to just what is written is to mutilate it, to cut it off from its sources. To so reduce the Word is purely and simply to kill it. Over the ages, in all the Jewish and Christian communities that have produced biblical texts, no writing or discourse has come into existence with which the Word could be identified. The Word is an event, a creative act, the subversive practice of a living person ever at work throughout history. We cannot fix or freeze it; we can only follow it, or rather, we can only follow him, walking in his footsteps.

In Diagram 2 (see page 44) a circle is inscribed within a triangle; let that circle be "the space of the Word." It is to be found in the text or begins in the text and is articulated in a practice that the text elucidates. It is a word that circulates; it is not fixed— dogmatic, doctrinaire, alienating—but is active—free, creative, new—summoning hearers where and how they are. Not just a sign or sound, not a set of "how to" directions, not an ideology, it is something—someone!—initiating movement, radiating. As one militant group reports it, "The one to whom it happens tells the others." So it has been with the Word of God from the beginning: it happens to someone who manifests it, communicates it, and tells others about it.

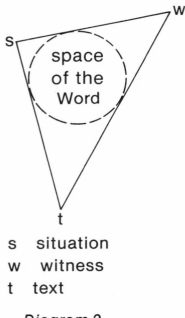

s   situation

w   witness

t   text

Diagram 2

In Diagram 3 (see page 45), in addition to the circle within a triangle formed by one situation, witness, and text, we now have another situation, another witness and, consequently, another text and, therefore, another triangle. With that, the space of the Word is changed, is no longer the same. Yet the "wager" of the witness of scripture, and even more of the Jewish and Christian communities, is that, albeit with much hesitation and variation, there does exist between these different triangles and circles a certain coherence—that of the "successive practices of the Word." Continuity is maintained in the spiritual understandings of life, in the theological interpretations of existential experience, and in the "confessions of faith" worked out in time and place.

A person of the tenth century telling about the creation would probably have the same thing in mind, I dare say, as a person of the fifth century, but they would express it differently. Other times, other words: a basic principle of scripture. Not one message or one theology is to be found in scripture but messages and theologies, because there are different situations and different witnesses. The "wager" that the church makes is that through these messages and theologies and a succession of ways of living them out, there is continuity in acts of faith, a continuity that, throughout the centuries, is maintained, developed, and reformulated. This continuity never fails to lead toward Jesus Christ, the center who gives meaning to history—its beginning, its continuation, and its end.

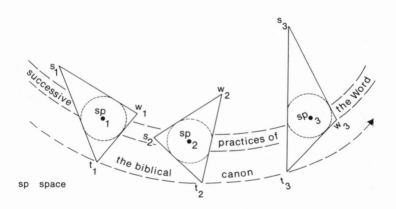

Diagram 3

The problem is that witnesses belong to a particular class and have made a class option and are not, therefore, neutral. If they represent political or religious powers, how do they "practice" the Word? Do witnesses represent oppression victimizing the weak, and are they then the bearer of an anti-Word? Particularly, what is to be said of those who, by serving the palace or the temple or some newly erected ecclesiastical authority, have played a decisive part in sorting out the texts and closing the canon of the scriptures? What status should militants accord to texts excluded from the collection of writings formally acknowledged as necessary references? This knotty problem lies at the heart of a materialist reading of the Bible and of all the analyses of passages that refer to the same situation but contradict one another. The experience of militants and the wager of faith is that, in spite of everything— as earlier writers put it, *hominum confusione et Dei providentia*— neither monarchical ideology nor clerical theology have succeeded in stifling the authentic elements dominating the biblical compilation: the account of successive acts and messages of liberation, the contestation of ideology by counterideology, the main thrust of which, from one era to another, passing through and beyond much faltering and failing, carries human beings from exodus to Easter, bringing them to discover the new humankind, encountered and confessed in Jesus of Nazareth.

This means that, if class conflicts occur throughout the biblical writings, the practice of the faith, articulated in militancy, strives to follow the course chosen by God. We shall come back to this point later on; it is as yet far from evident. Be that as it may, what has just been said shows clearly the dividing line between this search and traditional theology on the one hand and, on the other, certain extremely negative positions. The countertheology outlined here is distinctly different from a number of antitheological positions, it being understood, nevertheless, that a fundamental opposition exists between traditional theologies and all forms of contestation born of militancy. These have many nuances but constitute a single front of rejection and unalterable opposition.

Contemporary Readings of Scripture

In Diagram 4 contemporary scriptural readings are indicated by broken-line triangles. Since the closing of the canon (established by solid-line triangles), the content of the sacred writings has remained unchanged, but there have been untold myriads of new situations and new witnesses. The present generation has a different relationship to scripture than that of the biblical witnesses who, one after the other, read and reread scripture and

related it to their time, all of them in turn writing their interpretations of their own life experience. Contemporary witnesses—and
here we come up against the chance that the church takes, the risk
of the "scriptural principle," which has been termed the
"Achilles' heel" of the Reformation: the exclusion of any "infallible" magisterium entrusted with giving an authoritative interpretation of scripture—just as those of each generation since
the apostles, see themselves in the line of the successive practices
of the Word contained in the Bible from one end to the other.
Their problem is to find somewhere a point of access to this sequence and to reflect on those practices with care, caution, modesty, and originality in order to find a linkage with their own class
option in the world of today. There is no room for mere memori-
zation and repetition; what is needed is inventiveness combined
with fidelity, creativity and imagination combined with authenticity.

The original witness was not neutral; neither are contemporary
readers; their reading corresponds to their practice, to their class
options. Just as one practice is opposed to another, so will one
reading disagree with another. Once again, what is decisive is not
some method that would—almost magically—guarantee a correct reading, but the relationship between reading and social
praxis. Enough has already been said here about the inclusion of
traditional theology within the extensive register of the dominant
ideology and about the praxis of militant Christians that leads to
the emergence of a countertheology, which often seems to make
no small contribution to a people's struggle for liberation.

In summary, it can be said that, if the redaction of canonical
writings empirically came to a halt at the end of the apostolic
generation, the movement of the practice of faith that, in spite of
all the interventions of the powerful, gave birth to this canon,
cannot be stopped, because history, with its signs, direction, and
fruitfulness, continues to move ahead toward an end—the liberation and recapitulation of the universe. If, from the time when the
canon was closed, someone were to follow any other movement
than the spiritual interpretation of lived history, they would be
going contrary to what scripture means for the church in every
age. In other words, if "canon" signifies "rule," it allows us the-
oretically to draw a line of infinite extension. What is important
for a rule such as the canon of the scriptures is to draw a line that

can go on beyond itself. To use a modern image, the canon is like a rocket-launcher, pointing toward space it will send others to, although never reaching it itself.

All theology, like any other written work, begins *inductively*— that is, it begins when a witness or a believing community discerns the spiritual significance of some historical event. Secondarily comes a deductive moment, when the writing is reread in another situation by another witness, and enlightenment, direction, and inspiration take place. As will be seen, ultimately new readings by other witnesses contribute much to the general hermeneutic of the new historical situation. The dominant theology, by underestimating or rejecting the inductive phase of the whole process of writing, gives a work a nonhuman character, as if it were a divine oracle dropped from the heavens or a text formed outside the laws governing the elaboration of cultural documents in any age. Inspiration, the revelation of the Word of God, does not violate these laws; it informs and respects them at the same time.

From this perspective an analysis of some length and depth can be made of the story of Moses as given in the first three chapters of Exodus and the seventh chapter of the Acts of the Apostles to serve as an example. A baby of oppressed foreign workers is taken from the family (and class?) in which he was born and, for forty years, becomes a member of a royal family; they adopt him and introduce him into a new social situation. When he becomes aware of the institutional violence upon which his privileges rest, he makes a violent break with the Egyptian milieu, chooses a new social position, and becomes, for forty years, a foreign workman. Following this long existential experience he inductively evolves a new concept, a new name for God. During his forty remaining years, his approach is more often deductive.

The inevitable question arises, How are we to know what new writings will correspond to present situations and contemporary witness-agents? We must dare, we must have the courage to answer: they will be the reading, the analysis, and the "popularization" of liberation action that enables persons to free themselves from the economic, political, and ideological systems imposed upon them by the dominant classes, whether national or multinational. Martin Luther King, Jr., had no hesitancy in seeing this as the re-presentation and continuation of the exodus event in his own day. Assigned first place by the Jewish people in their credo as the key event of history, the exodus is the decisive principle for orienting and interpreting every personal and collective destiny throughout the Old and New Testaments. Liberation is not in any way hallowed as revelation, but when liberation is achieved, faith sees in it the action and manifestation of the living God. History is in no way divinized, but the believing community refuses to see in it nothing but the demonstration of immanent forces embedded once and for all in matter as the determinant of its evolution. On the contrary, the believing community takes the risk of finding historical possibilities for free and liberating actions capable of creating new possibilities and a new people.

In the past, those who, with a daring out of joint with their times, talked in this way about "faith events" were peremptorily condemned. As a matter of fact, it can be said with little danger of being wrong that the dominant theology focused more on their class option than on their "doctrinal deviations." Again today, those considered heirs in the same reprehensible family line are not only minorities but also individuals denounced and discredited—if they are not, in the name of "national security," handed over to the secular arm of military dictatorships. Elsewhere, in socialist countries, bureaucrats generally prefer representatives of traditional religion because they are considered less difficult to domesticate and more in conformity with the image of religion they wish to uphold and popularize.

Additional reasons exist for making it clear that the history of popular liberation and workers' movements for winning power and establishing a socialist society—with a human face, of course, and without concentration camps or psychiatric hospitals for dissidents!—cannot be ("open canon") added to the collection of biblical writings. But liberative militancy discerns throughout scripture the thread of the human adventure of those who have fought their way out of foreign captivity and exploitation in order to move on to a city of fellowship founded on justice. And faith, reading about the biblical exoduses and Jesus' liberating praxis, finds in popular liberation movements the echo and prolongation of a course of action that was particularized in the destiny of the people of the Old Testament only in order to illuminate and transform the destiny of the whole world.

There is then no question of making history a new "holy scripture," but neither should it be isolated from any relationship with the decisive struggles being carried on by human beings to win a future for humanity. Again, if scripture is "closed," history— that same history—keeps moving on, and faith is in danger of persisting in interpreting history today as it was interpreted in biblical accounts. The history of human liberation can and should be read as a continuation of holy scripture provided that it be fully understood that the circles inscribed in the triangles of the "new texts" *can be centered only within the borders within which there exists continuity in successive ways of living and practicing the Word* (see Diagram 4). The biblical history of liberations offers us a reading that is precious for the decipherment of the history of all the ages up to the present. This is the hermeneutic gamble taken by faith, which does not hesitate to affirm: such was once the practice of witnesses who declared, "The Lord said . . ."; and, consequently, such is our practice *today*: if God is not speaking today, God is dead!

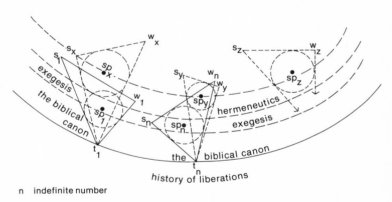

n   indefinite number

Diagram 4

(For contemporary rereadings, there are as many broken-line triangles and "spaces of the Word" for the same canonical writing as there are situations and witnesses—that is, an unlimited number—all of which have, nonetheless, the same point touching on "the biblical canon.")

Militancy and Christians

There is no conflict between militancy and faith. It sometimes happens that faith acts as one of the motivating forces starting militant action, but militant action has its own nature and rules; it organizes, becomes informed, and develops in accordance with them. Awareness of global reality—still infinitely diverse—and of class struggles; the analysis of techniques and systems of exploitation, oppression, and alienation; the endless search for a revolutionary theory and praxis better adapted to evolving situations that have changed from what they were originally and keep right on changing—all this cannot be deduced from faith, especially if faith, as is frequently the case, is nothing but the individualistic practice of religion as determined by the dominant theology. There is, on the other hand, a renewal, a transformation, or better, a first birth of faith when it becomes embodied in militancy as a praxis and achieves the unhallowing of the gods and taboos of power so that it becomes clear that, if God exists, God can *only* be a liberator.

There is no question whatever of establishing the necessity or the possibility of faith in militancy but simply of noting its presence and meaning. There are militant Christians—not militants because they are Christians (or this is less and less apt to be so, unlike Christians committed to "religious socialism" or "social Christianity"; in André Philip's words, "socialist because Christian"). Rather, they are Christian inasmuch as they are militant. What is more, they are not ashamed of it, but happy about it.

These militants are unconcerned with the famous "identity crisis" that has produced such a flow of ink and saliva in religious circles. They see it as the deterioration of a Christianity turned inward, painfully constricted in an attitude that attempts to defend positions lost forever, and not becoming involved in anything until they have defined, or attempted to define, its specific nature. Militants receive their identity from the regard that others—their atheistic or unbelieving comrades—have for them; all they ask or expect of militants is that they have the simplicity to be what they are, without pride or shame. Real revolutionaries are sufficiently aware of the difficulty of their enterprise and the danger of its foundering, and so they want the collaboration of persons of various ideological viewpoints, their only proviso being that all make their personal contribution to the same praxis and theoretical elaboration. In this spirit, the director of the Hanoi newspaper *Nahn Dân* asked Christians and Buddhists to unite with Marxists in a common effort to surmount the contradictions and psychologico-ideological obstacles blocking the progress of the revolution.

What does it mean to believe like that? It means having a particular and personal experience, which Paul Ricoeur calls "passing through the grid of the masters of suspicion—Marx, Nietzsche, and Freud." It means going through and beyond the criticism of faith as an alienating illusion on the economico-ideological level; as a transposition of a counterwill to power, the resentment of the weak toward the strong on the biological level; as a sublimation of the libido on the psychoanalytical level of the semantics of desire. "A Marxist critique of ideology, a Nietzschean critique of resentment, a Freudian critique of infantile anxiety are the routes that any kind of meditation on faith must travel."[15] They destroy nothing but the individualistic practice of religion prescribed by the dominant theology and in so doing make a contribution to purifying and radicalizing the reality of encountering Jesus of Nazareth. Indeed, in addition, militancy implies breaking with the dominant religion and theology, and so it divests this same Jesus of the cheap Caesaropapist trappings and all the lordly insignia with which the dominant classes have accoutered him, the better to make him a member of their own caste. It gives him back his true aspect as a man of the people, struggling together with his brothers and sisters, for integral liberation—inner and structural, temporal and eternal.

Praxis proves to be a decisive epistemological factor, a source of limpid, exhilarating spiritual knowledge. Rereading scripture within the framework of militancy imposes no arbitrary ideological framework upon it; it leads to rediscovering the right thread, the one that—above all, in the interpretations given of it by the dominant theology—has been so covered over that it is almost buried, swallowed up like the shepherd boy David under the paralyzing armor that King Saul wanted him to wear. We shall come back to this.

Believing is accepting within the very heart of militancy the summons of a word, an actual concrete word situated in time and space; it is accepting that praxis does not exhaust the ultimate meaning of things and, although basically it is not constantly called into question, praxis is continually critiqued and reoriented by coming in contact with the praxis of Jesus. Believing is accepting that his activity during his days on earth made a breach in our fate—that is, in all the paralyzing structures and categories of metaphysical, socio-political, and psychological oppression; it is accepting that what he has done has rid history of fate—that is, that he has given back to each and every person their rights, their opportunities, and their future; and it is accepting that his action has not been interrupted by death but continues throughout the universe today.

Roger Garaudy's remarkable "reading" of Jesus comes to mind:

All the gods were dead and humanity was beginning. It was like a new birth for humanity. I look upon the cross that is its symbol and I think about all those who have enlarged the breach. . . . For me, the power to create, humanity's divine attribute, is the host that contains the real presence every time that something new that will ennoble human stature is being born, whether it be love unto madness, a scientific discovery, a poem, or a revolution.[16]

Believing, as I see it, is discovering that an encounter with the living Jesus, far from toning down militancy, gives it roots, puts it in perspective, and, when it is in danger of wandering, brings it back in line—for example, when there is confusion between the principal contradiction, which sets the dominated against those who dominate them, and secondary contradictions, where the dominated are often at odds among themselves. Believing primes militancy, giving it new impetus when it starts to settle down and solidify, thinking that enough has been done with the first achievements of the revolution; or when it grows weary and weak in the face of opposition and failure; and when it begins to be satisfied by dealing with the structural, losing sight of the ultimate objective of every revolution, the cultural—that is, the transformation of relationships among persons and the transformation of persons themselves. Believing drives praxis to go more deeply into reality. Furthermore, and this is of capital importance, encountering the gospel delivers believers from the will to power, makes them loving and disinterested combatants, whose praxis is divested of concern for themselves and is fully integrated within the common cause, and they themselves are prepared for sacrifice, even to the giving of their own lives that others may live. If this truly is faith within praxis, it can be said without hesitation that militancy insures a faith that rejects the alienations of a dominant religion, just as faith protects militancy from being too short-sighted and too threatened by dangers from within.

The statement made at the conclusion of the first international meeting of Christians for Socialism in April 1975 in Quebec has the same thing to say. After making a deep analysis of world politics and the development of liberation struggles and before defining what a renewed church could be, it presents a brief statement of what a new praxis of the faith can be:

A New Practice of the Faith

15. In the context of transnational capitalism today, many of us have discovered that our living, reflection, communication, and celebration of faith in Christ find their true place in commitment to a liberating and revolutionary praxis within history. This discovery has led us to see more clearly that the revolutionary task is the place where faith attains its full growth and its radically subversive force. In taking up the task, we embrace all the demands of Jesus' practice and recognize in him the foundation of a new humanity.

16. The recent history of popular struggles, with their successes and setbacks, makes clear to us that the exploited classes and countries are themselves the first and true agents of their own liberation. On top of long-standing oppression, repression of a massive and systematic type is being carried out against every effort of the popular classes to transform the capitalist social order. The only effective and radical challenge to this combination of oppression and re-

pression lies in the struggle which comes out of the strength
and the consciousness of the poor of this world. Living and
reflecting on the faith in this context of oppression and repression forces us to seek untested possibilities in our testimony to the power of Jesus' resurrection. If the kingdom is
in any sense present when the poor are evangelized, we are
convinced that this occurs solely in the measure that the
poor are themselves the bearers of the good news of liberation for all people; that is to say, insofar as they make the
gospel their own and announce it in word and deed, rejecting the society which exploits and oppresses them. It is thus
that the "wretched of the earth" bear out their unresting
hope in liberation.

17. The praxis of the exploited is a subversive praxis
which seeks to build a new earth; to adopt this praxis is to
live the experience of an evangelical conversion and to find a
new human and Christian identity. Conversion means to
break with collective and personal complicities and to challenge oppressive power, above all if it claims to be Christian. It means to open ourselves to the burning question of
the needs of the popular struggle. This political and spiritual
rupture is the presence of the resurrection, the passover of
freedom, and the experience of the new life according to the
Spirit.

[One of the workshops at this meeting made the following
commentary: Conversion to the people and their struggles is
a specific way of expressing our conversion to God; God is
indeed self-identified with the hungry and the exploited.
This is for many Christians a decisive spiritual experience. It
is not simply an isolated encounter with the poverty of
Jesus, but an authentic experience of God at the heart of the
oppressed masses. And that is why to recognize the passion
of Christ—in a suffering people despised by those in
power—is already to be raised up by the force of the resurrection.]

18. Hitherto the faith has been lived and understood in
isolation from the contemporary revolutionary struggle and
in a world to which a conflicted and dialectical vision of
history is alien. Insofar as identification with the struggles

and interests of the popular classes constitutes for the Christian the axis of a new way of being human and accepting the gift of God's word, to that degree the Christian becomes aware that a faith-reflection rooted in historical praxis is really a theology linked to the liberation struggles of the oppressed. It is militant theology based on a choice of class. It uses the same rationality we employ to analyze and transform history. That is why Marxism is so important in this task of finding a new expression for our understanding of the faith. All in all, theology is verified by facts in the context of a revolutionary praxis, not mere words or new theoretical models, and that is what will allow us to avoid every type of idealism.[17]

The first workshops at that meeting offered a commentary that is appropriate here:

To spell out even more precisely our task of de-ideologizing faith, we can point out three criteria:

First, the criterion of *insertion* in the popular classes and their struggles, which alone can give a radical character to the analysis and denunciation of bourgeois ideologizations of the gospel.

Second, the criterion of the *social appropriation of the gospel*. A militant reading of the gospel is taking place at the grassroots level. The poor have the sensibility and the capacity of receiving and practicing the Word of God as a people.

The third criterion is *freedom of the Word*. We recognize that the Word of God is not totally imprisoned by capitalist utilizations. What continually happens is that the Word leads many persons to take up the revolutionary struggle.

Our faith is less ideological the greater the social function of our interpretation of the faith. By being on the side of the exploited classes and their struggle, our faith is characterized by the utopian rather than the ideological. The task of de-ideologizing the faith is a challenge to Christians in capitalist as well as socialist countries.

The gospel truth is under construction. To bear witness to the truth means to make the promise of sonship and brotherhood true, by transforming history from the grass roots, from the midst of this world's poor.[18]

At this juncture, we can rediscover the place of theology and return to St. Anselm's classic definition, "It is not enough to believe; I must understand what I believe." Or: *Credo ut intelligam*: "I believe so that I may understand." Theology is simply an understanding of the faith. In that case, contrary to what some others would want us to think that St. Anselm's dictum means, it does not seem to be the constitution of a body of logically articulated doctrines but an explication of my believing, acting, behaving, and evangelical practice at the core of revolutionary praxis.

Not only will this "theology" not have all the characteristics of a countertheology, bringing to light the complicities of the dominating theology and unmasking the socio-political roles it has played, but it will claim not to have any of its characteristics. It will be rather fragmentary, occasional, provisional, and strictly "local." It will have no pretensions about being perennial and universal. Yet it will have a role in continually illuminating the coherence of the reading of the gospel with praxis, the coherence of that reading with the original intention of the biblical authors—a critical and enlightening impact on praxis.

That a place exists in this context for properly theological reflection should be clear. According to Duméry's apt saying, "faith is not a cry." And the faith of a militant could not be more sentimental, diffuse, and unformed than that of a traditional theologian. If faith is responding to a word, it is also taking a chance on meaning. And militants cannot spare themselves in searching for a coherent formulation of the relationship between the meaning of their praxis and the meaning of their faith, both articulated in history, its risks, its hopes. Paul Ricoeur has said, "Christians in the world of today must be prophets of meaning." To put it in another way, faith corresponds to a reading of the real that allows for a dynamic line of conduct, for forging ahead toward a clearly perceived end without necessarily having a clear knowledge of all the different stages along the route.

"Arise, leave your country, your homeland, your father's house and go to the country that I will show you." The praxis of faith begins with Abraham, the father of all believers. A land is to be given to him, but he knows nothing of the steps that will take him there. What is important, what is faith, is to leave, to start out. Faith does not mean to possess but to take a chance; it is not stationary, but continually advancing. Whence Jean Cardonnel's whimsical statement, "I have no faith, and the best proof that I have none is that I believe"—because the act of believing is the antithesis of owning a religion. Jean Cardonnel is right, the act of believing—I should say "believing" instead of "faith"—is a tentative reading of the rushing torrent of life, an evangelical interpretation of praxis and the theory that praxis creates, that then orients and corrects praxis. Luther would have said that it is just the opposite of being securely sure; the only certitude is the risk of a whole life set in motion by meeting Jesus living in his word.

So then, "It is not enough to believe; I must also understand what I believe." Expressed within this way of defining the faith, theology seems to be an effort to work out an organic articulation of the different forward thrusts in the practice of faith. Experiences are analyzed, events are interpreted and related, history is given meaning and ordering from a global viewpoint, and a chance is taken at summarization. Finally, scattered events are directed to an end that gives meaning to the whole journey—to its beginning and end and all the stages of the way.

If the dominant theology, most of the time unconsciously—and with so many contradictions between practice and theory!—finds itself on the side of the criminal rationality of imperialist systems of oppression, countertheology, by giving an account, when that can be done, of the faith of militants, takes up a position on the side of the liberating rationality of popular struggles. We should not conclude from this that these two are alike. As the religious aspect of the dominant ideology, traditional theology, generally speaking, performs the function of justifying the established order. According to the disturbing witticism of Hans Hoekendjik, "Now these three things remain: faith, hope, and love, but the greatest of these is—the status quo."

A Latin American theologian has put it another way: "The best preaching, the most brilliant theological expositions, lead us to intone, *Gloria Patri et Filio et Spiritui Sancto.* And we come away edified, transported, resolved, *Sicut erat in principio et nunc et semper et in saecula saeculorum. Amen!"* This is the nobility and the powerlessness of Christian idealism in every epoch.

Unlike bridge builders, who submit a new structure to a final "overload test," traditional theology does not put any serious pressure on systems of domination. As a black theologian said to his white colleagues at Geneva in 1973, "At all times it is important to prove that the structures are holding up and not collapsing. Most 'political theologians' are always prepared to provide some repairwork inside the structures, but the structures themselves cannot be fundamentally called into question!"[19]

The theology that voices the rationality of militant faith has no such justifying function. Contrary to traditional systems, it hides nothing about the conditioning and social roles of "Christianity" but, on the contrary, does its utmost to throw light on everything. It is not the religious "yes, but" of the established order but a resolute "no" to its practices and values. If it gives an account of a living faith and a reading of the gospel that is being reenacted in radical militancy, this is to point out its possible incoherences, its inevitable weaknesses and limitations, and to furnish spiritual elucidation and criticism within the praxis of class struggle. Besides, conflict between classes has no need to be sacralized or justified; it is a temporary necessity brought about by institutional violence; it does not aim to keep on going indefinitely but rather to disappear after the establishment of a new society.

Pablo Neruda says, "I have never understood conflict save as a means of ending conflict. I have never understood harshness save as a means of ending harshness."[20] But his grand optimism leaves unsolved the problem of de-escalating the conflict and the harshness.

In summary, it could be said that, barring exceptions, traditional theology is articulated, is stated clearly, and gives an integrated presentation of the orders of creation, of an original era to be preserved and recovered, and of the omnipotence of an immutable God whose incarnation had the function of restoring what had been destroyed by rebel-sinners. Countertheology, on the contrary, draws its vigor from hope, has a positive and innovative stake in the future, confidence in the integral development of humanity in history and in its eschatological fulfillment. All this is rooted in the experience of an encounter that results in a new identity, radiating—with Jesus of Nazareth—the irruption in history of a renewed humankind.

Chapter 3

The Four Dimensions
of Hermeneutics

Collective Understanding

Hermeneutics is the science of Hermes, the god entrusted with clearly transmitting to human beings the results of the confused and stormy deliberations on Olympus. But as the patron of merchants and thieves, Hermes is also responsible for getting commodities across borders and from one culture to another and for using his influence to effect currency exchange. Finally, he is the protector of physicians, who are trying to restore the fullness of life to those threatened by death.

Hermeneutics, then, has four dimensions. It translates a divine message into human words (the task of the prophets of the Old Testament). It transposes what was said "at that time" (*in illo tempore*) into contemporary categories, looking for equivalent ways of expressing in one culture what was formulated in another. The work of biblical translators corresponds to this second dimension, particularly since we have come to realize that to translate mechanically, word for word, phrase for phrase, is impossible, and the trend is moving more and more in the direction of a dynamic search for basic correspondences. Translation becomes, in fact, a transmutation, and experience proves that an adequate composition on the language level can be attempted only when the translator dares to attempt expressing what the

original text means today. The third dimension consists in re-
claiming possession of the text and its meaning from those who
have unwarrantedly locked them away.

Still memorable is the stupefaction experienced by Luther
when, as a student at Magdeburg, he one day came upon a Bible
attached by a heavy chain to a desk and decided then and there to
release it and give it to the people. But since then scripture has
again been largely confiscated by clerics of all sorts, magistrates
who believe themselves authorized or, even more than that,
divinely appointed to give the only authentic interpretation of it,
professional exegetes with a scientific arsenal that relegates non-
specialists to the status of complete intellectual dependence. To
be sure, the impressive progress of biblical sciences and the
advance they have made possible in the fields of scriptural
translation and redaction are not only extraordinary but deci-
sively important for the history of theology. But who profits by
them, one ventures to ask, except for a restricted number of cul-
turally privileged persons who belong, as it must be, to the intellectual stratum of the middle classes?

And does not "ongoing formation," the newest and most positive enterprise of progressive theologians, run the risk, in spite of
all the precautions taken, of creating a new caste of "literates"
who will automatically have the power to instruct and direct
the people? That is the reason why there can be no question of
stopping at this stage with an enlightened bourgeoisie when
nothing proves—but rather the contrary—that their action
is more authentically liberating than that of the cynics of
wealth and power. If conscientization—that is "political alphabetization"—does not constantly interact with scholarly work,
serving as a corrective by popularizing it—by letting the crowd get
hold of it!—then this fine effort will remain marked by the
equivocal—and finally negative—mark of the dominant culture.
That is why the third dimension of hermeneutics is its most vital,
its most indispensable constituent, because it involves taking the
text away from its thieving possessors and giving it back to the
people.

To do this is not impossible, but it requires that the commentator and exegete make the social breakaway and undergo the conversion referred to earlier. In 1971 when the Protestant Federation recommended, by a narrow majority, that parishes, groups,

and movements study the document entitled "Church and Powers", it caused a widespread and salutary disturbance, as mentioned above. It is true that what the memorandum sought was unusual enough to seem provocative:

> Churches are requested to question themselves sincerely regarding the relationships that they in fact maintain with economic and political powers in place, and to ask themselves what kind of relationships would be consistent with their mission.

To many the problematic seemed really obscene because it completely exposed what must always remain hidden. And, rightly or wrongly, readers criticized in all sorts of ways the historical and economic information given, as well as the authors' style and lack of tact and moderation. To a considerable degree, these criticisms were so many alibis to avoid questions in depth that readers refused to address. Yet one day after an explanatory report had just been given to a workers' community, an old man got up and said, "This is the first time that I have ever heard the church speak my language." What the bourgeoisie could not and would not understand, militant workers accepted quite naturally, recognizing in a certain number of the document's assertions a class position similar to their own.

True hermeneutics is therefore situated at an entirely different level from the very respectable and indispensable level of reading techniques. For one who has studied, even just a little, Bultmann's discourse on the categories of existence as a key to the modern interpretation of biblical texts, it is a shock, but not a surprise, that the key to a credible modern interpretation of biblical texts for a person completely removed from the fascinating research work of contemporary hermeneutics is not some ideal definition but real life shared in fellowship with others. To put it another way, if, at the utmost, exegesis can be purely scientific, neutral, and objective, hermeneutics is always partisan; it is authentic only by being really popular. This conviction is basic to Paulo Freire's "political conscientization by alphabetization."

Decisive consequences could result: the end of the magisterium of exegetes, called upon in the future to join with militants (and supposing the exegetes were also militant!) in searching for a meaning that exegetes would have no chance of finding alone. The customary sequence of exegesis-hermeneutics is under review. Praxis and practice are the sources for interpreting history and historical texts.

In addition, academic hermeneutics is untrue to itself to the extent that it concerns itself much more with personal existence than with history and insists on the individual dimensions of understanding and faith. Here is what Ricoeur, one of the most lucid contemporary specialists in this area, has to say:

> What we have here is a circle: to understand the text, I must believe what the text imparts; but what the text imparts to me is given nowhere else save in the text: that is why it is necessary to understand the text.

The central place of the "I" and "me" in this passage should be noticed, showing, as it does, that the person in question is a reader of philosophy, an exegete, and a believer. It is necessary, moreover, to distinguish between the "I" of personal experience, the communal "I" of the psalms, and the methodological "I" used in this instance, which could be abstract—that is, with no place in history and no position in society. He goes on to say:

> A circulation is created among all forms of demythologization as it originates in philosophy and the demythologization that proceeds from faith. One after the other, the modern person, then the existential philosopher, and finally the believer heads the action.[1]

It is to be understood that "these three are one" and in certain regards as solitary and self-sufficient as a trinitarian god. Elsewhere Ricoeur says:

> . . . in the modern human being a believer and an atheist are at war with one another; in the believer, a critical adult opposes a naive child listening to the Word.[2]

Ricoeur's research, as honest as it is demanding, has given us too much to be lightly rejected. Yet it is becoming clearer and clearer to me that it is deficient because it is too individualistic and foreign to the collective development of humanity. In that progress Ricoeur has, in other respects, taken a significant part. Bultmann, Ricoeur's pedagogue in this area, can be regarded as the most authentic but also the most tragic heir of the theology and, even more, of the solitary spirituality of the pietistic traditions coming down from Luther to Kierkegaard.[3] How often history can be ignored or—what is more serious—not integrated in hermeneutic research. A simple fact, a single date bears witness to this: in 1941, when the Third Reich was making an all-out offensive at the heart of the U.S.S.R. and the cremation furnaces in concentration camps were being daily crammed with their ration of Jews, communists, and other deportees, Bultmann launched his manifesto, *The New Testament and Mythology*, in which he explained that the New Testament world of spirits and miracles had become decidedly foreign to the modern scientists and technologists who were in control of themselves and of the world. His exposition was all the more disconcerting because, unlike Heidegger, his master in philosophy, Bultmann had always been a resolute anti-Nazi, courageous enough to be prepared to pay for his stand with his person.

Fernando Belo has taken Bultmann severely to task for this enterprise:

> Bourgeois exegetes, working on the basis of anthropocentric logocentrism, have sought with varying success to undo the closure of the MYTH codes that plays in the New Testament texts. The name of Bultmann especially is connected with this attempt at demythologization. For a symptom of the fact that the attempt is being made on the basis of bourgeois logocentrism I need point out only the appeal to "the modern consciousness," to scientific reason, and to advancing modernity that seems always to be the ultimate argument in texts aiming at demythologization. This effort at demythologization fails to understand the scriptures and the narrative of power (the messianic narrative). This bourgeois form of the theological discourse ends up in *interiority* (even if it be called spiritual experience or a spiritual attitude), and it makes no difference whether or not the exegete be a "believer," as Bultmann is. These exegetes may talk about "the history of salvation," but in fact history has

been dissolved into the timelessness of consciousness and interiority and its relation to the "eternity" of God.[4]

The key to this evaporation of historical reality is found in the fundamentally negative attitude that Bultmann has toward the Old Testament, the part of the Bible where the changing, the provisional, and the political are taken seriously in their specificity and presented to readers as the setting for an authentic service of God.

The fourth hermeneutical dimension is "medicinal." It consists in allowing writings to revive that, like any documents of the past, may "die" or at least may retain only a purely archeological value. Only the dialectic of exegesis-hermeneutics, fidelity to the past and present, rootedness in tradition, *and* creative inventiveness can allow the resurrection of the living and prevailing Word, which is the center, the meaning, and the gamble of each rereading of the biblical texts. This "resurrection-insurrection" of the Word is the great adventure experienced and longed for like a grace by every hermeneutist who serves a people struggling for its liberation.

The Coherence of Readings

If revolutionary praxis is a starting point and an inexhaustible source for a new interpretation of reality; if, in contrast to the masking of de facto social relationships perpetrated by the dominant ideology, it makes an analysis of social structures possible by exposing their inhuman features; and if it prepares for the overthrow of those structures, then we can see that it is clearly the principle for a complete, authentic, and fruitful hermeneutics. Ricoeur states that "all of human existence is a text to be read."[5] Among the multitudinous ways this could be applied, I suggest, for our present purposes, elaboration of four interpretations:

i) An interpretation of the contemporary—and, consequently, past—history of the world; of the environment and trends in the particular society where the militant lives.

ii) An interpretation of the organization, power structures, and ideological influence of great ecclesiastical institutions, and of Christian marginal groups and their role in the micro- and macro-sociological environment.

iii) An interpretation of militant organizations, their strategy and tactics, their faith, their psychology, lifestyle, and self-understanding, personal as well as collective.

iv) An interpretation of biblical writings, starting with the social relationships characteristic of the societies in which the texts were produced in the successive periods in which they were edited, with particular emphasis on the motive forces operating at the time. Included will be a consideration of the resonance of this last area on the other three.

This is an undertaking that will never be completed, that will, therefore, be an enduring effort to analyze the whole of reality—in order to transform it from top to bottom. Obviously, each of these areas, conditioned by the others, reacts on them in a critical and creative way, and does so to a greater extent when militants use the same instruments on each of them, without reducing them to the same process or destroying or diminishing their specificity. Indeed, an integrated analysis is to be had through praxis. Thanks to it, it is possible to observe a particular class and to ascertain its position and to note how everything is organized, situated, and weighed, with nothing left out or interpreted according to one particular reading.

The unity of the hermeneutical process is sometimes verified in the dominant theology. The theologians of apartheid are a case in point, completely justifying a personal and political policy of racism. Sometimes, on the contrary, and in the majority of cases, contradiction exists between the conservative or reformist practice of theologians and their idealistic discourse, which seems to be the visible tip of that formidable iceberg—the unhappy religious conscience—a point of discord in apologetics, if it still exists, and a godsend for confessors, if there are any left.

Diagram 5 is an attempt to give a presentation of hermeneutical circulation. This differs altogether from the circle of interiority in which modern human beings, existential philosophers, and naive believers shut themselves in and dialogue with themselves. Passing through ideology and politics, it moves from the more universal to the more personal, from the economic to the "spiritual."

If the question is raised, "Where is the Holy Spirit to be found in all this?" the answer is obviously that the Spirit can be operating everywhere, or that, if we try to reserve the Spirit a special domain, the Spirit is not there at all!

That many militants have begun by reading scripture and by a praxis enlightened and guided by the practice of Jesus bears repetition here. The important thing is, I daresay, that they ultimately discover the primacy of praxis in their enlightenment and that they move from a particular religious level to a universal and universalizing hermeneutics, within which religion too has its consistency and specificity. What is essential, in any case, is that there be circulation, and that we be ready to experience how it enriches the understanding of scripture and of the de facto situation. In Diagram 5 the broken spiral lines indicate progress in the hermeneutics both of the de facto situation and the institution, and of militants and scripture.

Hermeneutical Circulation

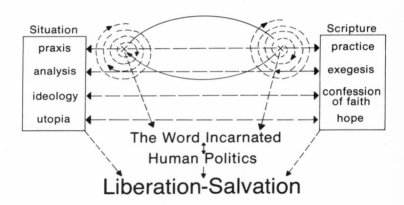

Diagram 5

—*All the lines, curved and straight, indicate continual movement, tension, challenge, and dialectic.*

—*The schema excludes "politics derived from scripture" as well as "scripture derived from politics." The two poles dare not be confused.*

—*Whatever the starting point of lived experience may be, the dialectic of the "inductive" and the "deductive" becomes evident.*

—*The general situation represented applies to the community as well as to the individual, to the lay person as well as the cleric.*

—The schema relates to any theology. The dominant deductive theology ignores or repudiates it. The inductive theology of militants recognizes it as in accordance with reality and wants to make maximum use of it.

Out of regard for symmetry—which is not arbitrary but in conformity with reality—four levels in each of the hermeneutical processes are indicated:

i) *Praxis*, which needs no justification: class conflicts and the decision to break with the established order provide the grounds for its existence. *Practice* is born of experiencing an encounter with the living Jesus and the existential decision to follow him.

ii) *Analysis*, which relates to praxis and reinforces its character as a permanent principle for understanding the real; *exegesis*, which is a reading of texts born from practice, but which in turn becomes a mainstay of practice.

iii) *Ideology* (in the Leninist meaning of the term: an overall interpretation of the whole world in view of the revolutionary seizure of power) and the *confession of faith*, which is the discovery of a meaning of the gospel in relation to each situation where it is to be made manifest; successive confessions of the faith over the centuries simply serve as examples and do not function as constraining models for Christians today.

iv) *Utopia*, which provides a midpoint and the ultimate attainment of militance, just as *hope* does for all Christian practice.

Clearly, we do not have to identify the two terms of these pairs or look for some accord between them. Actually, in some circumstances they may possibly be at odds with one another and they are certainly *always in tension*. My wager is that this dialectic will always be productive and rejuvenating, and will contravene dogmatization and oppose shutting the door on life and change; that it will strike at the roots of clericalization and bureaucratization; that it will stand for the ongoing renewal of practice and praxis, of the revelation of the gospel and revolutionary progress.

I have no apologetic intention here, nor do I seek to justify any sort of revolutionary orthodoxy; all I have in mind is to take seriously the simple fact that *militant Christians exist*. This means that praxis does not paralyze evangelical practice, and that evangelical practice in no way counters a people's struggle for liberation but is normally and necessarily integrated with it. That this is not always so in fact, even today, is patent. At this stage, a number of Christians—the Paraguayan priests and the Vietnamese Christians after 1951—have been so conditioned by the dominant theology that they think they must choose between the faith and the fight. From the perspective outlined earlier, participation in combatting the powers of exploitation and oppression is the very framework within which Christian practice will find full development and renewal in the original dynamics of the gospel, not forgetting that the gospel is completely expressed only in both testaments, the Old insistently reminding us that everything is political, and the New, which does not contest this principle, but emphasizes that politics is not everything.

Partisans and Gospel Readers

The true origin and real productiveness of the dialogue between Marxists and Christians have followed a similar pattern. If, in the passage of time, such dialogue has become a luxury or the occasion for some intellectual Christians to experience and communicate to their audiences a pleasurable thrill, originally it took place in a common praxis, the French resistance to Nazism, engaged in by those who believed in heaven and those who did not.

After a liberation that was incomplete (I can recall with some bitterness the motto ''From Resistance to Revolution!''), because it was only national and not social, the two sides continued to meet because, although they had started from different ideological positions, they had taken part in the same struggle and had become credible to each other. They kept on challenging one another, explaining themselves to each other, engaging in the essential dialectics of making a political critique of religion and a theological critique of ideology (''theological'' in the sense of ''messianic,'' of openness to the future and rejection of all dogmatic and bureaucratic scelerosis). Diagram 5 schematizes this dialectic.

Dialogue was choked off because the two sides became divided over a concrete issue, the 1968 intervention of the Warsaw Pact forces in Czechoslovakia. It has been resumed in proportion to the degree to which old partners and comrades have given up pretending to be infallible and have allowed themselves to be challenged in some depth. It began timidly but kept on, becoming freer and broader.

The evolution of the exchange is significant. At first it dealt in a learned fashion with each other's fundamental principles; later on, an attempt was made to turn Teilhard de Chardin's "common front" into a plausible reality. At the present time it deals with common undertakings for the good of humanity. In this respect, Italians and Vietnamese are in the vanguard, although, among Marxist critics and militant Christians alike, there are some who are distrustful of the mutual questioning involved in dialogue.

This alone should make short work of certain suspicions or even calumnies. It is impossible to recognize any truth in the statement of a conservative writer who stigmatized "those who think that the essential mission of Christians consists in establishing a new society by having recourse to violence if necessary."[6]

What is interesting and typical is that force is condemned only when it is directed against those who have been exercising force against millions of others. In bourgeois literature, it is customary to decry revolutionary action on the pretext that it will certainly "wreck the economy" and institute "a bloodbath," although at the same time passing over in silence the appalling economic and bloody crimes committed by the imperialist powers, whatever their names. It is also distressing to discover the extent to which the position of those considered to be potential dangers to society and to established values can be misrepresented.

The position maintained here is that the vocation of Christians is to be "prophets of meaning." Prophets of a particular meaning, of one meaning, would be putting it more exactly. But Christians will not be taken seriously if there is not coherence between their revolutionary praxis and their evangelical practice—not blended into indistinction but coherent, neither antagonistic nor unrelated.

Meaning cannot be explicated from without, from outside the borders of class conflicts; it is engendered from within, as many examples prove—for example, Martin Niemöller, Martin Luther King, and Camilo Torres—even though they were authentic products of the dominant theology in their own countries. Where a real break has not been made, there is no point in talking about meaning and prophecy. Practice that contradicts theory makes nonsense of meaning.

Proponents of all sorts of positions extending along the whole spectrum of the traditional front are often at odds with one another, but agree in arguing against a hermeneutics of biblical texts through a reading of reality. They say it ends by distorting the gratuitous character of the good news of the gospel, transforming it into a new form of legalism. It would be well for these critics to reflect upon the yoke, the straitjacket, of standardization that centuries of compromise, with indeed prostitution by, power has imposed on the dominant theology and, through it, on the Christian masses.

Apparently there is an understanding of grace—the "cheap grace" denounced by Bonhoeffer—that holds that, provided we believe in Jesus Christ and receive pardon for our sins, everything else is, if not a matter of indifference, at least secondary or even insignificant. This does not mean that Christians would be free to accept the world as it is. Today almost nobody maintains such a radically "spiritual" position. (We leave it to others to practice because, when it comes to our own rights, we know how to battle for them.) But Christian freedom would then consist in treating symptoms rather than attacking the roots of evil. And, as it is often put, is not evil, is not sin impossible to eradicate this side of the last judgment? And so we will always have with us until the end of the world the poor and the rich, injustices and wars. But it is an outrageous sophism to attribute to historical realities such as poverty, underdevelopment, and slavery a natural and permanent character. They are the direct products of contingent, changeable structures. The same sophism encourages a relatively passive theological attitude toward the social and interpersonal manifestations of sin on the pretext that they will be extirpated only with the resurrection of the dead.

The apostle Paul took a vigorous stand against those who accommodated themselves to the exterior manifestations of sin, maintaining that grace would then be in some way constrained to superabound (Rom. 6). Again, in this regard, it will be said that the trend is in another direction, that we have left behind a theology and pastoral ministry centered on "the beyond." Indeed, just listen to the average sermon heard on the radio or on television or even at Sunday services. Look at the voting statistics of practicing Christians, even if they are undergoing some change. Ascertain to what degree racism affects daily conduct. In these matters, as in most others, the behavior of Christians is indistinguishable from the behavior of the rest of the uncaring and reactionary portion of the global population.

Revolutionary praxis, with all its Promethean risks, takes seriously the war that God has declared on all those who visit injustice and violence on others and sanctify military glory, the police state, and a religion of wealth. Our one obligation is to refuse to regard history in a way that contradicts God's set purpose and to do all that we can—without self-satisfaction or an easily contented conscience—to achieve at least a minimum of conformity with a God who stands on the side of the poor, the enslaved, the oppressed.

It is understandable that those who compromise and collaborate with capitalist imperialism, with a world of multinational corporations and multimillions of starving persons, who limit their protests to words, militancy seems an intolerable mandate. It exacts a high price, and it is accompanied by a never ending awareness of being always behind in working out the tactics to correspond with a stated strategy. The compromisers and collaborators justify their stance by an appeal to anticommunism, which, under more than one title, can be considered the fundamental tenet of the credo of Western Christians and by the pathological satisfaction they experience in face of the unacceptable deformations that they find on many levels in socialist regimes. Even when shortcomings are taken into account, we cannot fail to recognize that what is at the root of all this is a firmly embedded, *a priori* rejection.

As "Che" Guevara, following St. Paul's lead, well understood, what is at stake here is "the law of love." No one can impose that law on someone else. Those who have encountered Christ have freely taken it upon themselves, as did those in the gospels whom he called to himself. Levi, Zacchaeus, the rich man, the adulterous woman, the centurion—all understood that to follow him meant changing their lives in the concrete areas of money, sex, and civic morals. St. Augustine was to illustrate this by saying, "Love; then do what you will," a maxim not meant to foster an arbitrary ethic but to encourage strict congruence between hands and feet, eyes and heart. If the heart is loving, how can the body, the whole person, with all its human functions and activities, do anything else but act lovingly? Camilo Torres had the same thing in mind when he said, "The duty of every Christian is to be a revolutionary; the duty of every revolutionary is to work for the revolution."

"Political Conscientization by Alphabetization" (Paulo Freire)

Bourgeois hermeneutics is bogged down in positivism and interiority. The reading of biblical texts together with a dialectic of practice and praxis makes it possible to gain a new understanding of the chief elements of the gospel. Ricoeur recognized this when he wrote, "At one and the same time, everything works together in complete reciprocity for an understanding of the Bible and of our times."[7] A real understanding of the Bible is to be found in history, politics, and praxis; a real understanding of our times becomes articulated through the biblical message, through living as a disciple, through praying. And the great myths found unacceptable by existential and historical interpretation will recover a new validity as soon as they are inserted into a political reading of revolutionary praxis.

An extensive work would be needed to deal with this important topic. Here are some of the material it would include:

—the creation of the world, which will be considered at some length in the following chapter;

—the fatherhood of God, the object of all the attacks of a superficial Freudianism;

—transcendence, even though it is neither a biblical term nor, in the strict sense of the word, a biblical theme;

—the negative character of the world, particularly as it appears in Johannine literature;

—the resurrection of Jesus;

—eschatological expectation and the eschatological event.

CREATION

Collectively, human beings are ecologically and politically responsible for an environment that they are capable of destroying.

If it is destroyed, the cause will lie with human beings alone. Humankind has at its disposal everything needed to reorient it for the welfare of all.

FATHERHOOD AND TRANSCENDENCE

If God is liberator, then the divine fatherhood and transcendence (the fact that God precedes, passes through, and continues beyond personal and collective history) are integrally subordinate to divine deliverance. The father slain in psychoanalytic theory would be, biblically speaking, the devil! What is more important than anything else is that Jesus (and the revolutionaries who follow him) is not a Promethean hero. The meaning of his existence, of his selfless service, and of his sacrifice lies in his integration within a plan over which he has no mastery. True militants are humble and heedful beings who accept having their immediate ends shaped by others, who recognize the ephemeral span of their own activity and the modest character of their role as links in a movement that began before them and will carry on after they have gone. The political hermeneutics of divine fatherhood and transcendence provides Jesus with real practice, shields him from any suspicion of arbitrariness or proud aloofness, and puts emphasis on a fundamental dimension of militancy—conversion, breaking with the will to power on both the personal and the institutional level—with what Latin Americans call *caudillismo*, "bossism." To be sound, a revolution must have these characteristics.

In general, the Johannine texts regarding the fundamentally evil character of the cosmos—that is, of humanity rejecting the work of God and the work of Christ, hating Jesus and his disciples "because its own works are evil" and because they are "in" the world but not "of" the world—have been interpreted in a purely ontological sense. A theology of hope—a political theology founded on a promised reconciliation—has often been obstructed by a (false) dualistic interpretation of some scriptural texts.

A reading of militant practice, on the contrary, reveals that the world "given" to humanity is a world that has become evil: within it dictatorships, gulags, torture chambers, oppression, and hunger reign. There can be no question of coming to terms with that world. It hates those who are "in" it but not "of" it—that is, those who refuse the structures and ideologies of domination and have committed themselves to stand up against it in revolutionary struggle. Like Jesus himself, the militant must realize that the cross is the price of the battle waged not to destroy the world but to do away with its "princes" for the liberation and welfare of the people. There is no doubt that a revolution is not going to set everything right, . . . but . . . one day at a time.

RESURRECTION AND KINGDOM

In Jesus militant faith encounters, besides his sacrificial role as an active liberator, a living being. It recognizes him as one who illuminates all history, who proclaims that every defeat is only temporary, that those who have given their lives for the future of humanity live in the praxis of militants. We must not give in to despair, to fear, or to resignation: these are the dominant classes' best weapons against the people. *¡Hasta la victoria siempre!"* "Onward to victory!" "We will fight until the enemy is overcome!" "Che" Guevara's rallying cry is the motto of every revolutionary. Authentic revolutionaries must be prepared to forego seeing the new society, the new humanity, for which they fought and have, perhaps, given their life. A successful end to the conflict is assured and, with the establishment of a classless society, human relationships will be qualitatively different and the coming of justice and equality will make reconciliation possible at last. The revolutionary gamble is that life will triumph.

A hermeneutics based on dominance diminishes and attenuates the message of the scriptures, reducing it to the idealist and the existential—that is, to the individualistic dimensions of conservative ideology. A political reading of the Bible does full justice to the historical and universal actuality of its great myths.

Praxis looks only to the engagement of the masses, whereas faith relies also on the fulfillment of a divine promise. What is accounted for by effort on one side, is attributed to God's grace on the other. Yet as long as the time for militancy lasts, praxis will not change or, to put it more accurately, praxis will be situated and judged by the whole hermeneutical process analyzed earlier. The fact remains, however, that time will tell. The eschatological surprise it will create will be almost as great for one group as for the other. What causes frowns and the setting aside of Occam's razor for experts of the dominant theology does not trouble militants. They have something else *to do*.

Chapter 4

Reading in Tune
or out of Tune
with the Times

The Death of the Armchair Theologian

Texts for a nascent countertheology, even though sketchy, tentative, and awkward, are beginning to form an imposing collection. Their production is relatively recent. It was only in 1968, when the theology of development was beginning to be criticized, that Gustavo Gutiérrez, when calling attention to the necessity for liberating action to oppose existing national and international dependence, ventured to use the expression "theology of liberation," which thereafter became well and widely known. An ambiguous term, it seemed to indicate that a new theme had been found like those that had surfaced earlier—such as "a theology of the world," "of revolution," "of violence." It was, however, *another* theology, another way of reading the gospel—through practice, the practice of engaging in struggle for liberation.

As the Peruvian theologian has expressed it, it is an attempt to reflect theologically on *the aspiration for liberation*, an effort to read it with the eyes of faith—that is, to exercise judgment and discernment about it:

To judge and not to justify blindly. To read a historical event or a human aspiration with the eyes of faith, not wanting to approve them as such, but trying to discern what good they contain. Judgment means discernment. It is the role of the Word of God.[1]

What is of prime importance—the acid test—for this counter-theology is that it must have nothing to do with playing the part of an onlooker. It must form its judgments of an action from within that action and in solidarity with its ends.

Few guides are to be found in this field save for those opposed to us; the task is hard for those who were totally or partly formed in their schools. Nonetheless, it is possible to find a certain number of historical reference points, without going so far as to canonize "heretics" of every variety burned in God's name by the dominant theology. These include, at the end of the Middle Ages, the Waldenses and the "Poor Men of Lyons" and those following an enduring current of Czech theology from John Huss, martyred at Constance in 1415, to Josef Hromadka, who died in 1969 during the "normalization" following the "springtime of Prague." For him authentic faith was inseparable from the revolutionary transformation of society. To more than one theologian tempted by a conformist interpretation of Barthian orthodoxy, Hromadka has communicated both the decisive motivation and the means to undertake the needed rereading of Barth's works. Then there are the reforming Methodists and nonviolent Quakers, both groups indefatigable challengers of the established order. Add to these the currents, largely deductive in their approach, of social Christianity or religious socialism in Germany, Switzerland, and France during the nineteenth century and at the beginning of the twentieth.

Finally, there is Karl Barth. Recent research has established socialist militancy as a consistent characteristic of his thinking for half a century and has, as a consequence, brought out the inductive character of his theological origins. All this was largely obscured by two sets of circumstances. On the one hand, Barth was led by his professional activities to construct a remarkable deductive system completely polarized by the struggle against National Socialism. This prevented him from pursuing socialist activities on both the theoretical and practical level. On the other hand, the dominant theologians and the ecclesiastical powers, having an inkling of the danger represented by an outstanding man who refused to be confined in the accepted political, academic, and ethical framework, took steps to reclaim him. Barth's socialist activity and the socialist positions that he embraced until the day of his death[2] were minimized as eccentricities, appendices, bits of folklore that he saw fit to add to his neo-orthodox works. As a result, conformist theologians and pastors could declare themselves "Barthian" without in any way calling into question the structures and values of social orders and ecclesiastical establishments. Here lies the reason for the astonishment of those who rediscover the young Barth today. How is it possible, they want to know, that his closest disciples could so misrepresent and emasculate him, and make him appear so bland?

Recently, and within liberation movements especially, first in Latin America, including Cuba, and then in Africa and Vietnam as well, faith is being renewed and lived in revolution. Adherents of the declining dominant theology in Europe are paying close attention to these phenomena and the development of a Third World theology. In the midst of the vestiges of a great past over and gone, they have a certain fascination for something they see as exotic. Their attitude as parasitic spectators has been highly irritating to those who have done original theologizing at the highest cost to themselves. In 1973, Hugo Assmann, a Brazilian and a former Catholic priest, expressed his thoughts along this line while in his second place of exile:

Having observed that discussion about the theology of liberation has run wild, perhaps it is important to keep in mind another observation: when, in the life of a people, things happen that are much more significant than what is happening, or not happening, in theology, that is one good sign that these occurrences—fragmentary, provisional, lacking in abstract theoretical consistency—are going to have greater resonance than do theological treatises. Perhaps the most positive aspect of the tremendous repercussions of our Christian babbling in Latin America is precisely this: they are a testimony emanating from a determined struggle against capitalist oppression. If this character is what is awakening interest, then we must be true to it. That means, in effect, that our writings are not to be taken as a purely theoretical exercise; *that our works are not to be transformed into a commodity to compensate for any sort of weakness* [elsewhere in the world]; that the little we succeed in doing is not to become an object for onlookers to speculate about; *that no one projects an image of Latin America in compensation for unproductivity elsewhere;* that, finally, each one of us in our own context joins the same determined struggle.[3]

Third World theologians meeting at Dar es Salaam in 1976 had the same thing to say at the assembly there and to European Christians as well:

We reject as irrelevant an academic type of theology that is divorced from action. *We are prepared for a radical break in epistemology which makes commitment the first act of theology* and engages in critical reflection on the praxis of the reality of the Third World. . . .
Our conviction is that the theologian should have a fuller understanding of living in the Holy Spirit, for this also means being committed to a lifestyle of solidarity with the poor and the oppressed and involvement in action with them. Theology is not neutral. In a sense all theology is committed, conditioned notably by the socio-cultural context in which it is developed. The Christian theological task in our countries is to be self-critical of theologians' being conditioned by the value system of their environment. It has to be seen in relation to the need to live and work with those who cannot help themselves, *and to be with them in their struggle for liberation.*[4]

According to Hugo Assmann, the theology of liberation can gain a hold when persons have passed the point of having doubts and discussions about:

—The possibility and necessity for a break with the capitalist system in spite of its power and notwithstanding the exigencies of a socialist solution. (Up to the present moment of history any such solution has remained largely unrealized and, when realized, partly betrayed.)

—On the international plane, an intensification of the class struggle between the Third World and the world of wealth.

—The widespread "domestication" of numerous expressions of historical Christianity by the capitalist system, which imprisons them within the system.

—The possibility and necessity to liberate from this captivity some important sections—but not all—of historical Christianity through a dialectic of continuity and discontinuity that will preserve the essentials of the Christian tradition.[5]

The hard challenge addressed by these texts and a number of others to European theologians has done much to discourage their kind of idealist flirtation—whether cool or warm—with Christian revolutionaries of the Third World. At the same time, European Christians of the left have been led to reexamine their practices and to envisage possible reformulations of the faith. To date, results have been slight. Confrontations in Latin America, if infinitely more dangerous, are much more clearly defined than those in Europe. Then, too, the fact that a number of Latin American theologians have their roots among the people makes their options more obvious, if not easier.

In Europe, the fact that most "conscientized" Christians belong to the middle class obscures uprootings and ruptures there inasmuch as the politico-economic upheavals needed seem more unlikely. Their consistent and effective praxis retains, in spite of the efforts of militants, an unremittingly ambiguous character, to the extent that their revolutionary strategy must be channeled through reformist tactics. Hence the debates about whether certain courses of action condemned to remain reformist reinforce or undermine the system. Frequently movement ahead is made tentatively, on the basis of uncertain decisions. It is not surprising that things are seen more clearly in Italy and, above all, among Christians emigrating from Spain because of work or politics.

A Materialist Reading

A time of darkness has to be lived through. A difficult passage must be made from one type of solidarity to another, and the break between them is not clear. We cannot hold onto the categories and methods of the dominant theology, we cannot be at home with classic liturgies and celebrations, but, at the same time, we do not have new formulations and frameworks to turn to. Life is led in a social, intellectual, and spiritual no-man's-land. Like Moses in the Midian Desert we wander, more or less lost, on an arid journey. Those of us who have dared to undertake it may not have to persevere for forty years, but it can be long enough to discourage and exhaust us. The thought comes to mind that, after all, Egypt's equivocal religion, once rejected, may be preferable to this emptiness, this paralysis, this death of faith, this end of sharing in the word and in prayer that we sometimes sense or meet among those who have gone before us in this exodus.

Many groups, many couples, have come to a halt at the threshold of militancy because they lack the courage to face the emptiness of Holy Saturday, when everything of the past is buried and the future has not yet dawned, and when they stand alone among their shattered certitudes, relationships, and community practices. Yet is not the grievous and glorious mystery of death and resurrection the basis for the revolutionary utopia of the oppressed masses? Is it not at the genesis of Paulo Freire's risk-taking conscientization? At the center of the apostolic proclamation of baptism? At the heart of the gospel of Jesus?

Sometimes the poor of the Third World are astonished on becoming aware of the extreme poverty of their rich oppressors and, when faced with it, they have no desire to adopt models in which the richness of being is swallowed up in the poverty of possessing. They turn away from pseudo culture and "our" multinationals, but reject even more categorically the existential void that becomes more and more apparent behind its protective ideological smoke screen. The oppressed, in their suffering and anger, in their hatred of classed society and their legitimate counter-violence, are still aware of who and what they are, but oppressors, unwilling to renounce their privileges and profits, their genocidal regimes and torture chambers, no longer know what it means to be human. They have lost the look and the identity of human beings.

The Third World puts an anguishing question to us: Is there still a chance that you will come back to yourselves? Will the poor have enough perseverance, enough generosity, and enough strength to liberate the rich?

There was an instance of it on April 25, 1974, when military officers put an end to dictatorship in Portugal. Inasmuch as they proclaimed peace for the Portuguese African colonies and democracy for Portugal, the poor of the Third World (Africa) and of the First World (Portugal) can be said to have inspired the first attempt to liberate Europe.

Wealthy nations, including some that profess to be socialist, immediately offered assistance to imperialists in order to bring Portugal back into their camp, the camp of possessors owned by their possessions, by their own nonbeing, and by their refusal to establish just relationships with the poor.

It is of special significance, then, that the whole of dominant theology has been sent reeling by a burst of impertinent laughter from a bearded Portuguese, an ex-priest, a migrant worker, and the author of the first European work of countertheology, Fernando Belo. His work is capable of restoring hope to the Third World for the future of Christianity in Europe. A difficult book, *Lecture matérialiste de l'évangile de Marc* (*A Materialist Reading of the Gospel of Mark*), became in a few months in 1974 the best-seller of a Catholic publishing house. It results from a risk taken—on good grounds—to "make possible a confrontation between a political practice that aims to be revolutionary, and a Christian practice that no longer aims at being religious."[6] This work is an attempt to adopt a faith-militancy dialectic and to garner its fruits through a rereading of the oldest gospel. In doing this, it shows no romantic dependence on Latin America or any inferiority complex in its regard.

I have no intention of repeating here the main points of this text. They irritate and disconcert professional theologians, and they excite and rally groups of lay persons. It should be sufficient here to refer to the numerous commentaries and criticisms dealing with it,[7] and then to underscore the following three aspects:

1. As a piece of writing, it cannot be understood unless the risk at its source is existentially accepted. Anyone who tries to do otherwise falls straightaway into idealist dilettantism. For his part, Belo freely utilizes the treasures of bourgeois science in order to make them bear fruit in another setting and for other ends than those for which they were intended. So did the people of the exodus make use of the treasures of Egypt!

2. The materialist method is in no way reductionist or myopic; it gives to the entire body of biblical texts its roots and contours, and pinpoints the functions within the social formation that produced it. It makes it possible to gain a better comprehension of a certain number of essential facts, such as the role of the temple as well as the relationship between Jesus and the Zealots. In addition and above all, it helps us to grasp the nature of biblical unity; seeing it not in uniformity but in the confrontation of contraries and a clear resolution of class conflicts by the sacrifice and victory of the poor.

3. In this work, much more than in innumerable treatises on christology, the person and action of Jesus stand out with arresting force and specificity. His messianic practice naturally challenged the established order and opposed clerical power based on the dominant theo-ideology. The subversion that he achieved was done by bodily, not theoretical means. With hands and feet and eyes he opened a whole new future for humankind. His practice affects the whole human being, and is the source, the standard, and the energy system of authentic ecclesiality—which is none other than the presence in history of militant disciples:

> Access to [the BAS, "basileic"] *circle* is had only by way of a *conversion* that is articulated according to two times: a time of a *break* with the SOC ["social code"] . . . and a time of following Jesus and taking over his practice of service and salvation. . . . What is the effect produced by this BAS circle? A fructification in blessing that is superabundant

. . . as one becomes one of the *poor* by sharing their bread (without any rich people). Break, following, fruitfulness: these are the three components of a messianic or ecclesial *conversion.*[8]

Clerical power will make every effort to imprison Jesus in a straitjacket of theological definitions. As Bonhoeffer put it, Jesus is always betrayed with kisses, even with theological kisses. But his dynamism bursts bonds.

Need anything further be said about theology at this point? Undoubtedly, a certain return to the deductive approach can and ought to take place, but only when the inductive approach has been clearly defined and the countertheology plainly positioned as a weapon of ideological criticism, born of and sustained by praxis, to be wielded *against* the dominant theology and *for* an authentic revelation of the gospel. If messianic practice is, following Jesus' lead, a liberating action for bodies together with an unhallowing of the orders of death as an irruption of communicable life, then it has its own logic and consistency. Its subversive creativity and unforeseeable originality can be "spoken" if they are first experienced. Reason is delivered from enslavement to ideological idealism and will be prepared to turn against the whole alienating arsenal of the religion of power. Countertheology is at the service of the messianic; it is called forth and put to work by the messianic.

As one cannot recite Gutiérrez, one cannot repeat Belo. If the fields are to be flooded, the dikes must be opened and the rereading must be done to correspond with the new epistemological principle—the practice of making a break.

The material that follows is only an illustration of what has just been said, an example followed by some partial and provisional conclusions.

An Attempt at a Materialist Reading: Genesis, Chapters 1 and 2

We are dealing with two conflicting accounts, which cannot be harmonized. The accounts have been located in space and time, even if the traditions, set down in writing as fixed, were formed bit by bit a long time before the final work of the redactors.

Our reading will be done on four levels: the geographical, the historical, the ideological, and the prophetical.

THE GEOGRAPHICAL

Verses 1:1–2: 4a present the first environment to be described. It is Mesopotamian, and the problematic is that of holding water in check, controlling floods and flood damage. Verses 2:4b–25 present the second environment, which reflects the arid land of the Negev and the problem of irrigating the desert. The god of the first account is a dredger of polders; the god of the second is a seeker of oases. Both deal with the "water/land" coupling but the "friend/enemy" relationship is reversed.

The writing uses environmental categories. The culture and experience of a people struggling for survival are crucial for the message to be understandable and credible. In any case, these factors condition the production of the text in a conclusive way, coloring not just its form but its whole vision of the things of this world and its conception of God.

THE HISTORICAL

The second account was probably drafted about 950 B.C. (a date used in a number of present-day introductions to Bible translations, such as the ones in the *Jerusalem Bible* and the *Common Bible*). It seems to reflect the material prosperity and stability of the Solomonic kingdom. The risks and uncertainties of the period of conquest are over; the state is consolidated, its power well established; its citizens know security. An administration of some size is set up in which the name of two "secretaries"—Elihoreph and Ahijah—are included in the list of officials (1 Kings 4:3). They are charged with setting down in writing the royal orders, with keeping the archives, and doing the work of historians. In this favorable climate is born the first great school of biblical writers, customarily called "Yahwist" (J). In a relatively euphoric atmosphere, when Jerusalem was extending its authority from the north to the south of Palestine, with the temple as its center and a unifying ideology for support, the Yahwist historians were given the mission to recount the glorious history of the kingdom and its monarch and, in addition, to conscientize the people so that, by its work and military courage, this remarkable political entity would last beyond the time of this exceptional reign. The schism of 933 B.C. is proof that the people did not succeed in that undertaking. Yet a nostalgia for this period of good fortune always had the power to reawaken the hope of the people, especially during and after the exile!

The first account belongs to the period around 500 B.C., the time of the return from the Babylonian exile. It was produced during a difficult time; the worn-out "remnant of Israel" finds life exhausting. Everyone thinks only of making a home for themself. Any collective tasks such as rebuilding the walls of Jerusalem and, particularly, rebuilding a modest temple, count for far less than the protection and promotion of personal interests. Then too, religious fervor and the consciousness of a specific national identity leave much to be desired; they become less and less palpable as the Hebrew people comes into contact with other peoples brought in by the conquering Assyrians. Mixed marriages and religious syncretism were the plagues of an epoch of disillusioned mediocrity. In vain, apparently, did the prophets do their utmost to reanimate the will to live and a feeling for the covenant, the core of their fathers' faith. The priests did assure continuity: through them the rites and principles of Judaism came to replace the spirituality of the exodus and the building of a new society. This first creation account is the fruit of their labor, a "sacerdotal," or priestly, document (P).

THE IDEOLOGICAL

What needs to be done here is to bring out the dominant ideas of the texts, and to ask ourselves what interests they express and serve, noticing how both sections attest to power—the first, priestly; the second, kingly.

The second account is a humanistic document. Unlike the first, it treats of earth *and* heaven; it proclaims the glory of man, the male, the sole and solitary head of the universe—the king at Jerusalem, the father in the nuclear family. To be sure, his limitations are emphasized: a product of the impregnation of matter by the divine breath (2:7), he lives and rules in a garden of the Near East (v. 10), where precise restrictions are put upon his power. He is not all-powerful (v. 17); he is—and he is only—the first of creatures in dignity and seniority. Having dominion, however, does not serve to dispel his loneliness and so, "for the first and last time," he becomes pregnant and from this unique pregnancy, terminated by a surgical intervention under a general anesthetic, woman—*wifman*—is born, the last in the chain of living beings, another being like himself, a helpmate to put an end to his cheerless isolation (vv. 21–24).

The four rivers referred to in Genesis 2:10–14 have been the cause of such an outpouring of scholarly ink that, were it water, it would make the desert bloom! As a matter of fact, there are no rivers marking the four cardinal points of the land and no currents flowing out of a mythical palace located in the far north. They are the two well-known northern rivers, the Tigris and the Euphrates, the Gihon, whose source is a spring in Jerusalem, the unknown Pishon—the latter too flowing in the direction of Arabia and the Gulf of Aqaba, tracing a kind of natural border. Inasmuch as the sea lies to the west and the desert to the east of the kingdom, only its borders on the north and south are uncertain. For the author of the second account, Eden is Sion and the heart of the "Solomonic paradise" (using the term as "socialist paradise" is used today); in the ideology of those days, the four rivers mark the extent that the empire was to attain.

Humanity, the people personified in its king—that is, in its appointed representative, the proprietor of everything living in the paradisiacal garden—may remain there only if the covenant continues to be observed. In the concrete, the Hebrews do this by carrying out the work of cultivation and defense, by being wholly devoted to guarding the land and making it fertile, using sword and plow in turn. They must be soldier-laborers (hence the use of the strong verb *abad,* meaning "to work as a slave"). There is no question of humanity's enjoying the fruits of the garden unless it wrings them from the earth, which it must continually regain from covetous enemies.

The second account is a text for mobilizing a people united around its king to wage a twofold battle for production and national independence; what is won must be preserved and enlarged without any letup.

The first account is a liturgical (antimetaphysical) text: from the start, "heaven and earth" indicate the perspective. Heaven is primary and its "light" antecedes the light of the sun (1:3) and makes manifest the truth of all things, while the breath of God broods over the hostile waters (v.2), elaborating an indecipherable universe and presaging an indecipherable humanity not yet present to attempt reading its meaning.

At a time when the worship of heavenly powers and astrology played a prominent part in the life of proliferating pagan cults and contributed, through religious alienation, to the resignation and passivity of the masses, some closed and permanent lines were mapped out: the *earth* is the center of all things, the outcome of a creative act, a place where humanity (male and female) exists in a three-dimensional relationship of God-humanity-nature (vv. 26–27) and works out human history. The stars, always divinized elsewhere in the world, are reduced to the ranks of "luminaries," instruments for human service, reference points for the days and nights of humanity. Each time that a limit is placed on cosmic forces that can threaten fragile humanity, the domain of "the good" and "the very good" is made evident. From the beginning, God's action is to give humanity a space where it is to dare living in freedom.

God did indeed bring an end to the disastrous deluge, just as God opened a path through the Red Sea for the people of the exodus and a way through the desert for those returning from exile. God is the original, the never ending, eschatological Creator. So it is normal and necessary for order to be created out of chaos, for a liturgical week to become the framework in which life will find meaning and limits. (It has been clearly proven that the authors of the priestly document [P] transposed a Babylonian series of ten days into a week of seven with the sole purpose of rooting the Israelite Sabbath in what some theologians call "the order of creation.") This order existed before the appearance of the human couple. They relate to God and God's deputy only by conforming with the Creator of space and time by scrupulously integrating themselves within the liturgical framework that the Lord of the earth has fixed as precisely as the movements of the stars through day and night have been fixed. This couple, this human community, fulfills its function only if, as "an image of the God-Word," it grasps and communicates what it lives in the framework of an order and values (the "good," the "very good") as defined by God. The priests are the true interpreters of the divine will; they are continually reminding the people of it and assure its being respected by placing the great Sabbath liturgy and its infinite ramifications above private interests and individual and collective transgressions. Integration in worship is the end envisioned by this text: only the sanctification of the whole of life can give it its true meaning. Judaism comes into existence and its clerical claims are stated in sweeping terms: those who wallow in the profâne place themselves outside the great living current flowing through history. Israel is not only the conscience and the light of the world but also the point of convergence for the human venture in its entirety.

The Sabbath is obviously a *political* fact. It not only commemorates, by its very existence, God's gift of time and space to humanity so that it could be free but it also has an anticapitalist, antislavery function as well (Lev. 25; Deut. 15). Even if these principles were largely trampled underfoot or, perhaps, rarely put into practice throughout Jewish history, they nevertheless represent among that people a utopia that never fails to call to account structures of exploitation and oppression. The narrative of the return from exile shows how incompatible with the celebration of the Sabbath is the forced labor put upon the lowly by the high-and-mighty (Neh. 13:15ff.). Liturgy is not an evasion of the real but its nerve center: all life is liturgy—that is, in the strict etymological sense of "a service of the people."

THE PROPHETICAL

A materialist reading neither destroys nor diminishes the texts; quite the contrary, it relates and unifies them. The first and second accounts appear as they were meant to be, not as "accounts of creation" destined to enlighten us about the origins of universal becoming but, under the guise of cosmogonies, with all their elements of mythology and demythologization, as interpretations of the meaning of personal and collective life. (According to Harvey Cox, the desacralization of nature has an antimetaphysical function.) The point of these two accounts is to communicate a political ideology and a global understanding of the history that they relate: the existence of Israel, the existence of anyone who takes the good news of the covenant seriously and is bound up with the action of God, whose breath makes matter and history fruitful. Human beings alone, among all animate and inanimate beings, can apprehend and express the truth of everything in space and time. The human being is an existential being, and whoever responds to the challenge to make an existential decision by giving to life its true weight and its real significance for others, becomes "a prophet of meaning."

What seems important to me, at least in relation to a working hypothesis for this study, is pointing out those elements in the texts that appear a contradiction of the ideological environment that produced and colored them. Although the texts are expressions of the dominant ideology, they have at the same time a surprisingly and obviously "counterideological" dimension.

In regard to what the second account tells us of royal power in the tenth century and what the first account discloses of priestly power in the sixth, we see, rather than evidences of power, an unexpected freedom, something that existed throughout the Old Testament and can be called the "prophetic" dimension of the texts.

Vis-à-vis the "great king," his officials, and all the authoritarian fathers in the society of that era, the second account makes the emphatic statement, "Remember you are but a man" (a refrain chanted several times during the coronation of a pope). The king of glory is called *adam,* a plowman, a clodhopper, a generic term recalling his origin and the necessity for him to remain humble, down to earth, close to the ground, a servant of the soil and of land, which he may not use just as he likes without losing his original roots.

"Original sin" consists in wanting to be like God—all-powerful. The king therefore is not the best and the greatest; his greatness and the greatness of his people lie in observing the strict limits imposed upon them by Yahweh. An absolute power based on divine right is categorically denied. As has been rightly emphasized, in all the states surrounding Israel at this epoch the king was a god, but in Israel God was king!

In a time of triumphant masculinity and general polygamy (think of the fantastic description of Solomon's harem [1 Kings 11:3]: seven hundred women of royal rank and three hundred concubines. Poor man! Poor women!), the Bible stresses that just one and only one woman is man's real partner. It is "not good" for him to remain alone; and it is in encountering his partner that he becomes himself: the word *'îysh,* "man," appears not before but after *'ishshâh,* "woman." The birth of the other reveals the man to himself. They are face to face, as close and complementary as possible to one another. Their relationship is not to be one of domination of one by the other but of complete reciprocity. In addition, in their marriage, the woman is the one who becomes the place and the home for man (v. 24); he is the one who takes leave of his place and his home to join her—against all the customs of the times. He is the chosen rather than the chooser. This amounts to a remarkable revindication of woman. Yet even today, all its social, ecclesial, and theological implications are far from being realized—in Christian communities and among militants as well.

In the first account, what is expressed is subtler but no less real. Nascent Judaism has put its strong clerical imprint upon it but, in the midst of the priestly function of creating and extending the sacred, there is expressed a stake in life—in the life and survival of a people. Hidden in every line of an apparently closed text is a passion for the future of that people. Furthermore, at the very heart of a legalism bent on imprisoning everything within its arsenal of moral prescriptions and religious rites, the good news resounds with the statement "I give you" (v. 29).

Even in the postexilic hierocracy, what makes life good and worth living is that it is a gift, a present, a favor. From beginning to end, what God has in view for humanity is what is good, very good. Genesis 2:18 expresses the same thing in a negative way— for man to be alone is "not good." And God makes the good life possible by giving human beings a world to enjoy. Even the priests could not prevent God from "making the sun shine on both the good and the bad, and the rain fall on the just and the unjust alike." This striking liturgical passage proclaims the gospel for the earth. The real reason for the law is human happiness. The lawgiver is *good* (Mark 10:17–18).

Above and beyond Solomon and the power of the clergy, the two accounts proclaim that God is the liberator of every human being. Because God acts in history, no power on earth is absolute or final. Those who read these texts can no longer be passive subjects of a king or submissive wards of priests: they have been called to become men and women who stand on their own feet.

It is surprising to find here, just as in the antimonarchical documents of the First Book of Samuel, obviously contradictory themes: "ideological" and "counterideological." How is it that the kings, the patrons, the rulers, the representatives of the people have been so poorly served by those whom they paid to celebrate their glory? How is it that catechumens with a spirituality of peasants understood dogmatic and moralistic priests better than the priests understood themselves? Doubtless it is because, as Marx and Engels clearly saw, every alienating religion engenders and evinces the antidote that partly counteracts its negative effects: the voice of the people is discernible in the writings of clerics and courtiers; it keeps crying out and, if it does not succeed in drowning out other voices, it persists; it is there, a fountain springing up from a countertheology that the dominant ideology cannot succeed in sealing off. Over and over again and in spite of accumulated obstacles raised by conformist exegesis and thundering doctrines, the oppressed of every age will come to draw from its waters.

That they do so will be attributed to the astonishing action of the Spirit, to liberating inspiration, no doubt. But it is also an unexpected and quite striking instance of the old adage, *Vox populi, vox Dei!* Could not a popular theology be formed by giving an account of what God has said through the aspirations and struggles of peoples oppressed by political and religious powers? That would be a worthy undertaking.

In his *Contribution to the Critique of Hegel's Philosophy of Right* (1843–44), Marx writes, "Religious distress is at the same time the *expression* of real distress and the *protest* against real distress."[9]

These two elements are to be found in the two biblical accounts under consideration: the people's submission to royal and priestly power, and its determination to move in the opposite direction toward a life unburdened by any constraint, toward a harmonious way of social living marked by equality and responsibility. Whether the world is organized by palace or temple power, both systems are found oppressive: human beings want to build a human world; they need to control their own destiny.

A Critical Balance Sheet

Where this reading seems to fall somewhat short is in being largely dependent upon the results of the historico-critical method, recognized as being a far too unreliable instrument in itself and, in addition, a product of bourgeois ideology. This is so, to be sure, but why not utilize the monumental work of biblical scholars in order to go even further and, more than that, occasionally to take the opposite tack? A free appropriation of the work of Gunkel, Lods, and von Rad, a rather less than scholarly reading of what they have already said, pays them the best of compliments: without knowing it, they have opened the way to a reading of these writings in function of the socio-economic factors that colored them and are indispensable for a materialist reading. A reading of this nature is indebted to them for groundwork without which it would be nothing more than arbitrary speculation and imagination.

On the other hand, is it not evident that ideology and counter-ideology serve as a very useful means for dating written works? If we cannot consider it as a strong probability that the second account belongs to Solomon's era and the first to the time when the Jewish people returned from exile, we must nonetheless grant that the second presupposes a politico-economic framework analogous to the one that was inaugurated by the establishment of the kingdom in Jerusalem, whereas the first suggests a priestly theocracy asserting itself in a syncretist milieu. A materialist reading takes up where the historico-critical method leaves off, correcting and confirming it and bringing out its true import.

If we accept Hans Heinrich Schmid's thesis in *Der sogennante Yahwist,* which dates to the sixth century the whole group of writings to which the second account belongs, they do nevertheless reflect the shape and ideology of the Solomonic kingdom as revived under Ezechias (716–687 B.C.) and Josias (640–609 B.C.), or as they still survived in the nostalgia of the popular religion. If this is the case, we would have a typical example of "ideological lag"—that is, of dominant ideas and the reactions that they evoke continuing to exist long after the politico-economic conditions that engendered them have passed away. All throughout the history of Israel and up to the New Testament, Solomon is always the glorious king (Matt. 6:29). Every subsequent king is identified with him and is a king only in Solomon's image and because "the son of David" comes again and lives in each of his successors.

A problem remains: What of the final redactor who, long after these two works were produced, incorporated them into a single whole? Are we to think that he did not see the contradictions between them and that, if he placed the first passage before the second, he did so because it offers a broader viewpoint, a more harmonious arrangement, a less exotic account? Or was he ideologically closer to the priestly rather than the Yahwist account and so used the priestly version as a decoding grid with which to read the following chapters? All this is but conjecture. There is also the hypothesis that the final redactor might have been blind to the radical heterogeneity of the two texts. That hypothesis can be calmly put aside, in view of the respect that persons of those bygone days had for anything in writing and the sacred character with which these particular scriptures were invested.

If one of these writings follows the other *without any attempt being made to harmonize them* at a time when in other instances signs of such efforts are apparent, was that because, for the authors of the Pentateuch, the reading of history operated in an either/or fashion in accord with the perfect and unchanging freedom of the Spirit and in relation to successive forms of the dominant ideology? At the end of the fifth century before Christ, did there exist a clear notion of the origin of oral traditions and of a way to fix the date of written works? No matter; it seems evident that, from the time when the biblical collection was begun, there was a desire to put the reader on guard against accepting it as a magical text that had fallen from heaven. The Bible is written and dated in close attachment to the successive epochs in which it was produced. For that matter, it is not texts, but the successive periods of the practice of the word that the Bible re-presents.

The two passages under discussion should be considered as two *examples* of how generations of the past were able to live, and as invitations to readers today, wherever they may be living, to dare to write new texts, at once dependent on these two and freely formulated for the present. And who could predict whether the first or the second account would then become more enlightening for us? How are we to talk about the Christian meaning of history and of respect for the land and for life when we are being threatened not by the desert but by urban cancer, when our problem is not to people the earth but to limit demographic explosion, and when not the right use of royal and priestly institutions but the seizure of power by the people is the subject on the agenda?

The intention of both authors of the two accounts—and of the redactor as well—is to define the conditions that make human life possible and ensure human happiness: the vision of faith regarding God's will on earth, and the meaning of God's action in history. Creation opens up space and time as an environment for making something good of life. That implies, because everything remains ever fragile and imperilled, that some rules and limits are to be maintained, and that the word of God is received and manifested as the source of life. Happily, no appeal is made to metaphysics: faith is down-to-earth practice; the eternal, the heavenly, is affirmed and confirmed in the matter of fact of everyday life.

Obviously, a materialist reading, far from emptying texts of their "spirituality," roots their spirituality in the real. A traditional idealistic reading often gives us a presentation that is as high-minded as it is untouched by any brush with time and space and is, consequently, ineffective. Materialism rediscovers the truly spiritual rooted in the concrete and refuses to relinquish a jot of it. Another quality of life is offered to those who, within the circumstances and limitations of their own history, accept the possibility of a liberating practice and, by that very fact, the promise of and the need for meaning in their personal and collective life. This is what the fourth Gospel calls "eternal life," a radically new possibility to be lived from this day forward, a stake in another world, a sign and a profile—like conversion itself—of the fulfillment of history.

Not surprisingly, a contemporary and legitimate interpretation of these texts is chiefly oriented toward overcoming hunger, surmounting nuclear dangers, and safeguarding the environment—tasks that claim priority—for those who confess faith in God the Creator. An appeal by Charles Birch, an Australian, at the Fifth Assembly of the World Council of Churches at Nairobi on December 1, 1975, deals with these questions:

> If the world is to sustain the lives of its four billion inhabitants and more to come, the world itself must be saved. But are we willing to pay the price of the redemption of the earth in terms of a revolution in values, in lifestyles, in economic and political goals, and even in the nature of the science and technology we practice? Or shall we continue with the Faus-

tian deal of "travel now, pay later?" The journey unfortunately is short. The time for payment has arrived. . . .

The creation stories are not about events in the past. They
are about relationships of dependence, alienation, and renewal in the present. The image of God as the artist who
painted the flower and left it is inadequate. In some way
God is involved in the being of the flower and in all that
exists here and now. We need a valuation of the creation
that has within it a hierarchy of intrinsic value (of human
beings as well as sparrows) and which includes the concept
of the rights of nonhuman nature. If existence on this earth
is to be sustained it may be by a perilously slight margin of
sensitiveness of those who value nature for more than its use
to us, in what Paul Verghese calls "the reverent-receptive
attitude.". . .

If we are to break the poverty barrier for almost two-
thirds of the earth's people, if we are to continue to inhabit
the earth, there has to be a revolution in the relationship of
human beings to the earth and of human beings to each
other. The churches of the world have now to choose
whether or not they become part of this revolution.[10]

There are many documents providing information on the Third
World that highlight the relationships between development/
underdevelopment and ecology. They are models for contemporary readings of these two texts of Genesis.

Ecological problems can be treated as alibis for problems that
are fundamentally political, or they can be an expression of the
ultimate consequences of such problems, on the level of the important choices of society that today affect the future of humanity.

Chapter 5

Labels and Uniforms

Geography, Class Struggles, and Theology

No better example of the far-reaching penetration of a dominant theology can be illustrated than by the two contrasting world maps on pages 100–101. To experience how a number of groups, including some in the southern hemisphere, react to these maps is very instructive. Faced with the second map, by Arno Peters, viewers are first disconcerted and then amazed: Why, they ask, has it been so completely distorted, with Europe all squashed together and Africa and South America so outlandishly stretched out? It takes some time and persistence on the part of an instructor to help them discover that this is the image that results *when the equator is centered on the map* and the true proportions of the continents are taken into account, following the highest German scientific authorities, such as Professor Carl Troll, president of the International Geographical Union.[1]

Centering the Pacific Ocean on the map adds to the strange impression it gives but, even so, it fails to work any transformation in the image of the world that we ourselves have and convey to others. We are too accustomed to seeing ourselves as "the center" and looking upon the white branch of the human race as dominating the continents on our periphery.

That the new map has been published by Weltmission (Evangelische Arbeitsgemeinschaft für Weltmission, Hamburg) is not fortuitous. As a group doing missiological studies, they are anxious to point out the distance separating evangelization from colonization, ecumenism from imperialism.

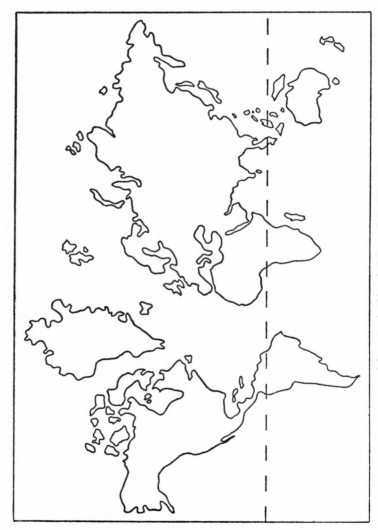

Mercator's Classic Map of the World

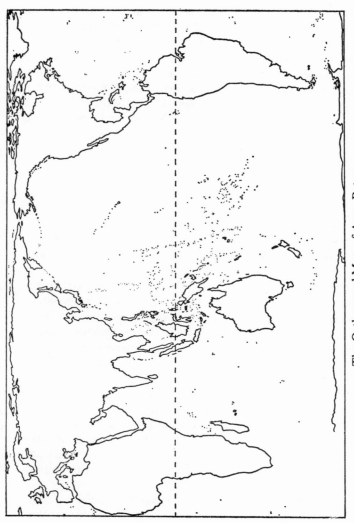

The Orthogonal Map of Arno Peters

Whites and, sadly enough, even one-time colonial peoples who have become independent feel more at ease with a geography of domination as represented by Mercator's map. And even if formerly colonial peoples are intellectually convinced of the correctness of the other map, they remain deeply attached—make no mistake about it!—to the image that the masters of the world have presented of themselves and disseminated among their subjects. We have here a telling example of what has been called "ideological lag," a sort of inertia in mental and psychological structures of domination that makes it possible for ideologies to remain in human minds even after the economic and political structures that produced them have disappeared.[2] Hence the evident necessity of working on all three levels—the economic, political, and psychological—at the same time. A revolution is incomplete if it does not penetrate to the cultural sphere.

Gustavo Gutiérrez emphasizes the same point:

. . . we are considering liberation as the *liberation of humanity throughout the course of history.*

To say so is to emphasize the fact that structural change is not enough to liberate humanity. To state that every human existence has a political dimension is not to claim that it has no other dimension.

To effect a definitive and lasting change, structural change is not enough; humanity itself must be changed. It has inner freedom and it must change itself, maintaining a critical attitude toward every social achievement because political liberation will not deliver us from economic dependence, the ultimate source of injustice. Nor will we find ourselves in a society where all will be well, where structures will not give rise to injustice. To believe that would be political naivety, to say nothing of a lack of faith. . . .

In Christian circles, the question is often asked, "What good is it to change structures if you do not change humanity?" And then the statement is added that "humanity has to be changed *first.*" I answer, "Are you able to change anybody independently of their social conditioning?" We cannot claim to change human beings in a social vacuum. Human beings do not exist in a vacuum. Aristotle says that human beings are political beings, social beings. Changing the human heart is done by changing the social conditioning of humanity.

We cannot say that we must begin, *chronologically speaking*, by changing humanity before we change structures; nor that we must change structures before changing humanity. . . . Changing structures does not bring about a change in humanity and changing the human heart does not automatically produce a change in structures. Yet *the two are closely related.*[3]

We are here touching on something that we must live and breathe day in and day out: the indispensable dialectic of conversion and revolution. If, in revolution, it is idealistic and illusory to expect the conversion of thousands of dominated persons, the personal conversion of the revolutionary does remain an essential contribution to the soundness of a great collective work, constantly threatened as much from within by its adherents as from without by its enemies.

This being so, it is important to clarify the relationship between class conflicts and Christian love. The first sentence of *The Communist Manifesto* of 1848 will serve as a nucleus for this attempt. It reads, "The history of all hitherto existing society is the history of class struggles."[4] The first thing to be remarked is the use of the plural—struggles. No dogma is promulgated, no abstract principle is formulated: a fact is stated. To talk about "class struggles" is not to resort to using a slogan but to point out one possibility for analyzing in depth infinitely diverse situations. It means entering into their concrete reality and examining how, in each case, conflicts between the dominated, struggling for their liberty and dignity, and the dominating, fighting to maintain and extend their privileges, have been determined and articulated.

In composing that first sentence during the mid-nineteenth century and in a European situation, Marx and Engels did not claim to give, once and for all, a general principle for all conflicts. They were offering an analytical instrument, a working hypothesis, that would make it possible for others to interpret conflicts, to find them intelligible, and to take a responsible position in their regard.

Were the two authors making a value judgment, an arbitrary statement, as has often been maintained? The question is important, but its answer has to await the concrete character of praxis. All things considered, perhaps the distinction found in classic theology between imperfection and sin can be of service here. Nobody has to be a Christian in order to know that humanity is imperfect and that its actions are tainted with error. Theology follows the scriptures, but goes further when it says that an imperfection, an error, that entails an essential break with one's neighbor and, therefore, with God is a sin.

When faith speaks of sin in its whole personal and social extension, is it just a matter of a religious expression or is it pointing out a constituent dimension of anthropological reality? And when we talk not just of "social conflicts" but of "struggles between classes," we are saying that, in the chaotic reality of confrontations between different social strata and occupations, a criminal kind of reasoning is revealed in the institutional violence that provokes counterviolence. Conflicts have a beginning and an end and, whatever external forms they may assume, they have the same underlying structural reality.

Marx and Engels, in the wake of other philosophers, used the notion of class struggles to formulate a value judgment on social reality. At the same time, it can be said—without proving it but illustrating and verifying it by many experiences—that they have also made us aware of a fundamental *fact* about the evolution of society and, even more than that, they have indicated a basic *law* operating in its evolution.

Bringing class struggles to light as a reality that qualifies all social conflicts on both the national and the international level can be likened to discovering some active but unnamed and unknown virus or bacillus causing an epidemic and resisting treatment by scientific means. The great era of exorcisms coincided with a period of medical ignorance, but the world of demons and evil spirits has now receded—spectacularly if not entirely!—as the therapeutic field of vaccines, serums, and psychological treatments has advanced. It could be that some Christians, impregnated by a simplistic anti-Marxism, are prolonging the reign of exorcisms in this post-Pasteur era and preventing scientific intervention in social conflicts by refusing to recognize what contributes energy and virulence to social conflicts. Once we have discovered the malignancy that is normally found in every social conflict and automatically rules out the possibility that it is something accidental, we are able to delimit the evil, name it, and strive to overcome it. What many do not recognize is that to qualify social conflicts as "class struggles" is to look forward to seeing them pass. We cannot reconcile ourselves to the idea that class struggles will never end. To take a stand on class struggles is to take a stand on getting beyond them to a time when all peoples will be delivered from oppression, whether it be the oppression they impose upon others or the oppression others impose upon them. And they will then know at last a full and final reconciliation. Moreover, to affirm this is not to deny other sources of conflict—racial, tribal, sexist, religious. It is an attempt to give them a common denominator in the analysis of conflict between oppressors and oppressed.

The Impossibility of Neutrality

Recognizing the impossibility of neutrality is imperative. It brings results, it makes it possible for us to emerge from the mists and darkness of those "nights when every cat is gray." Publishing a map with two-thirds of the world depicted as north of the equator and only one-third to the south is not an act devoid of guile: it implies enlistment in the service of the white Western system in order to keep it going. Using class struggles as a decoding grid to read "neutral" statistics, the most objective obtainable—for example, those of the United Nations—we substantiate the fact that the increasing distance between the rich and developed and the poor and underdeveloped is not dictated either by fate or by nature but results from a system that benefits one group by reducing another group to destitution. The widening gap between rich and poor has discredited every Western ideology about development and has cut the ground from under the comfortable apathy of middle-class Christians and the religious resignation of the poor masses. Countless examples confirm this reading of the conflictual reality present in the most diverse kinds of society.

As a working hypothesis, a scientific theory, or a law determining the history of societies, class struggles, whether hidden or obvious, are a constant in human collectivities, affecting them from head to foot. Far from losing their intensity, they are being radicalized in a spectacular fashion in the degree to which confrontations are hardening between the popular masses in all countries and the dominant structures, national or multinational. On the day after the Chilean coup d'etat in September 1973, Helmut Gollwitzer wrote:

No one can any longer ignore the class struggles taking place. When a class struggle is initiated from the top, it is an effort of the privileged to ensure their power as the dominant class, doing no matter what—from illegal and brutal actions to massacres—to achieve their end. When democracy can no longer guarantee their preeminence, they do away with it. Class struggles are not triggered by a handful of agitators or socialists. They are a constantly active ferment. When struggle begins at the top, it uses a variety of bloodless means and then, if need be, bloody means as well. When it begins at the bottom, it is the counterviolence put up by the oppressed. When anyone asks you what position you take on violence, first ask, "What is your position on institutionalized violence? On the violence of power?" If you are answered with hesitation, with irresolution, laugh off the question.

As Max Horkheimer expressed it at a time when his vision had achieved its greatest clarity, when we speak of capitalism, we are talking about fascism. This does not mean, as is often said, that capitalism could lead to fascism. It means that capitalism will of necessity have recourse to fascism when it feels that a situation is getting out of hand. In a recent issue of *Le Monde*, Léo Giulani wrote, "When unafraid, the ownership classes bear the look of liberal democracy, but when they become fearful, they show the face of fascism."

Our great minds today become very disturbed over the constraints put upon a few intellectuals in the Soviet Union. They even claim that the principle of noninterference, which they hold as sacrosanct when Thieu or Portugal are concerned, should be put aside when it is a question of Sacharov. Patently, they are just boiling up their same old anticommunist broth. We can have no doubt of that when we know how indifferent they are to the lot of intellectuals imprisoned in Greece and Turkey, two members of the North Atlantic Treaty Organization. And their approval of the Chilean putsch is strong evidence of their attitude. If they have to choose between a parliamentary democracy that leans toward socialism and a fascist dictatorship that opposes socialism, they choose fascism. Here is where a parallel exists between 1933 and today. This is why the whole world ought to know what to make of the fidelity that capitalist protectors have to the constitutionality that they claim they are safeguarding. . . .[5]

The "doctrine of national security," formulated in Washington in 1947 and carefully reworked and updated when the Cuban revolution of 1959 and the Chilean elections of 1970 shook dominant classes all over the world, is the most sophisticated and the most cynical expression of class struggles initiated at the top level. To win the war—cold or hot—against communism, the international enemy, the outrageous position was put forward that not peoples but nations exist. (Did not Goebbels say at one time that "the bigger the lie, the more easily it will be believed"?) Nations are then identified with the state apparatus and this is, in turn, placed under the strict control of police and military organizations—all civilians being potential traitors. At the same time, ideological control of the masses is entrusted to the central information bureaus and to the churches. The latter are charged not to stir up faith—with its capacity for critical and mobilizing activity—but to furnish the crusaders of Christian civilization with myths, rites, and symbols.

What we are concerned about here is not some distant, extraordinary event but an ongoing, concerted and concentrated, offensive against the peoples of the whole world. The worst imaginings of Orwell's *1984* are gradually becoming a somber reality for millions of men and women all over the world, not excluding Europe, where the threat is still veiled but is becoming more and more discernible every day.[6]

The duty of every sane and responsible person is not only to warn others of what is happening before it is too late but, more than that, to respond to the pressing, absolute need to resist an enemy infinitely more formidable than either Stalinism or Hitler's National Socialism. (In this context, no comparison of these two need be made nor need they be put on the same plane.) The unbending stance of militants often leads them to lose sight of the principal contradiction and they give all their attention to secondary contradictions among militant revolutionary groups, whose orientations and activities, however, are closely akin. For members of the same class to be at odds with one another is suicidal indulgence. The Chilean and Portuguese revolutions are two recent examples of this; both were weakened and immobilized by infighting. The only one who profited by it was the enemy. It is a paradox and a tragedy that activists can be convinced, subjectively, that they should fight their enemy and yet, objectively, they often play into their enemy's hands.

Almost everywhere the most "moderate" elements, the least conscientisized, are beginning to understand that neutrality is no longer possible, as the following statement of the Brazilian bishops, in their letter of November 15, 1976, impressively exemplifies:

Individual Security and National Security

We already said that the principle of equality of all persons before the law is the basis of any society that pretends to be civilized. Next, the security of each and every citizen of a nation is essential for its internal security.

The Brazilian Constitution affirms that "all power comes from the people and is exercised in their name." But to hear it said, on the contrary, that "it is the state that gives liberty and human rights" to the citizens, to the people, should not surprise us, if we keep in mind "the doctrine of national security," which has inspired the Brazilian government since 1964. It has given rise to a political system that is more and more centralized and therefore relies less and less on the participation of the people. According to the Christian and humanistic view the concept of nation summarizes all the ways in which people associate. The right of free association must be recognized, respected, and promoted by the state—that is, by the government. To be a member of a nation, however, does not mean to sacrifice trust, feelings, ideals, and values that may seem harmful to or even incompatible with the interests and viewpoints of the present political system.

Hence, according to the Christian and humanistic view, the nation is not synonymous with the state. Nor is it the state that bestows freedom and human rights. They existed prior to the nation itself, but the state has the responsibility to recognize, defend, and promote the human rights of each and every citizen.

Another great temptation of those who hold power is to confuse the duty of loyalty to the nation with loyalty to the state—that is, to the government. To place the state, the government, above the nation means to overestimate the security of the state and to underestimate the security of the individuals. That means reducing the people to silence and to a climate of fear.

Without popular consultation and participation, however, programs, official projects, and plans—even if excellent and successful materially and economically—easily lead to corruption and are not justified when they do not correspond with the needs and aspirations of the people. The ideology of a national security placed above personal security is widespread in Latin America just as it is in countries under Soviet domination. Inspired by it, regimes of force, in the name of the struggle against communism and on behalf of economic development, declare "antisubversive war" against all who are not in agreement with this authoritarian conception of the organization of society. Training for "antisubversive war" against communism in Latin America, besides leading to the growing brutalization [on the part of] the police, begets a new type of fanaticism and a climate of violence and fear. Freedom of thought and of the press are sacrificed; individual guarantees are suppressed.

This ideology has led the regimes of force to adopt the characteristics of communist regimes: the abuse of power by the state, arbitrary imprisonment, torture, and the suppression of freedom of thought.[7]

The degree to which the most traditional Christian line of thought can be changed when it refuses to remain aloof to what is actually happening in society is illustrated by the following statement by a group of Paraguayan priests:

So that you will not be at peace after hearing what we have had to say, we ask you: What side are you on? For centuries the fruit of the labor of the poor has always been taken from them through the socio-economic systems of the rich and they have been prevented from exercising their right to participate in the political and administrative life of society by repressive political systems. Structures have been established that necessitate oppression and dire want for their survival. Their continuation is predicated on the existence of a majority of exploited underlings and a minority of exploiters.

When the poor open their eyes in order to move toward deliverance, the social edifice begins to tremble. Those vibrations and the fissures that appear in the social edifice fill the rich, the powerful, and the bourgeoisie with fear. When the poor want to see and to move forward, the only reaction on the part of the rich is to blindfold them and put them in chains. (To block the vision of the poor, the rich wave before their eyes the phantasm of communism as a ravenous ogre that causes all kinds of calamities. However, that attempt fails to work, for neither the phantasm nor a real threat can prevent Christians from noticing the injustice and misery of the society in which they are living or from looking ahead prophetically to the world that they have to reconstruct.)

For us priests involved with the rural poor, this society not only sins against the poor but against Christ. "Insofar as you did this to one of the least of these brothers of mine, you did it to me." Prevent the poor from seeing, and you prevent Christ from perceiving reality. Keep the poor from advancing and you prevent Christ from moving ahead. We priests are not going to turn into atheists, but we are not going to use God's name to bless an unjust society or to exact a degrading conformity and patience of marginated persons. We priests are not going to be preaching violence but neither are we going to be accomplices of that institutional violence by which a great number of persons are exploited by a privileged few. We are not going to be accomplices in the violence of the powerful; we are not going to become their accomplices by being culpably silent. We priests will not be communists, but no silly fear of communism will lock us into a society that is neither Christian nor human. We are committed to going the way of change, and we will encourage humanizing change, whatever happens, and even if those with well-filled pockets shun us and call us communists.

In the name of the rural poor who are involved in their personal liberation, we ask you: What side are you on? We bring the message of the rural poor to this assembly: our master bears the name of Jesus Christ; he was born in a stable; he lived among the poor; he surrounded himself with sinners, laborers, beggars; and he wanted all to be free. He said that the earth was made for all, and that the fruits of the earth belong to all. He was crucified by the powerful of his time. Today he would be put in prison or placed in an insane asylum or shot as a subversive. He was, he is, and he will be with us, and we with him.

Being a Catholic or a Protestant, following this or that religion, counts for nothing if each of us is preoccupied with bettering our own life by trampling others underfoot. Becoming a priest or pastor just to stay inside the church, to read the Bible, and to preach sermons serves no purpose. It is worth nothing if millions of rural poor are treated like animals by those who come to Mass to find refuge for their souls.

While time is lost in words, in discussions, the arms of the rural poor are growing weaker, their labor is becoming more burdensome, their hunger is increasing, and their freedom keeps on being chipped away. If priests do not take a strong stand against the miserable state of the poor and take no part in the struggle to liberate them, then nothing that they preach is worth believing. If a pastor does not go out into the countryside to claim a small piece of land or a just salary for his poor brothers and sisters, the Bible is going to scorch his conscience. The words of songs and hymns are worthless if not accompanied by action to liberate the poor. No person should be the slave of another, no people the slaves of another people—because all are equal before God.[8]

This declaration is, theologically speaking, remarkable in the extent to which it shows what effect our participation in the people's struggles has on the image of Jesus Christ. In proportion to our praxis, his true image, lost through centuries of remodeling by colonial clericalism, is restored to us and to him. Once again he is a brother in arms, paying with his life for enlisting in the cause of liberation and inviting his disciples not to look for protection and security when face to face with those who scourge the poor and prolong the drama of his passion in history.

"Who Do You Say That I Am?" (Matt. 16:18)

Christology, the heart of theology, is, as we have learned, profoundly renewed by praxis. This will not surprise those who have really comprehended it and made the materialist approach their own. And there can be no doubt that, when this method of reading is developed and refined, there will be a better understanding of the reasons for the differences in the christology of different biblical books—the Pauline epistles, the Synoptics, John, Hebrews, Peter—and the successive definitions given by ecumenical councils and by tradition.

If it has been possible to speak of Jesus of Nazareth in terms of "the new Adam," prophet, son of God, Word incarnate, high priest, paschal lamb, and living stone . . . and, finally, to talk of him in the philosophical categories of "consubstantiality," "person," and "nature," is there any reason why he should not be expressed today in terms of liberator, man of the people, revolutionary—and in the categories of practice, class struggles, and social conscience? Great epochs in the life of the church have always come when enthusiasts broke away from the sacral and servile repetition of canonical writings and courageously launched upon the risky enterprise of hermeneutics. Dom Hélder Câmara challenged his listeners to initiate an undertaking of this nature in his celebrated conference of October 29, 1974, in Chicago when he asked the question, "What would St. Thomas Aquinas, the commentator on Aristotle, do if he were faced with Karl Marx?"

> To explain the importance of using St. Thomas as an example, I dare to remind you that today there are many thinkers who represent challenges, just as Aristotle did then. . . . Among several other thinkers who might be mentioned, Karl Marx challenges our courage because he is a materialist, a militant atheist, an agitator, a subversive, an anti-Christian. . . . If Aristotle's thinking only frightened Christians of those days, what should be our attitude today toward Marxist thought and, even more, Marxist practices? . . . As the University of Chicago chose to take upon itself the celebration of the seventh century of St. Thomas Aquinas, I suggest that the best way to honor the author of the *Summa Theologica* and the *Summa contra Gentiles* would be for the University of Chicago to try to do with Karl Marx today what in his day St. Thomas did with Aristotle.[9]

And yet, the archbishop of Recife cannot be ranked among the Christians for Socialism, or Marxist Christians, or materialist readers of the gospel!

It is both normal and necessary for the christology of militant Christians not to be like a foreign body within their dialectic of praxis-theory, not to serve as an element of "ideological lag" in contradiction to their revolutionary options, and not to be a ferment engendering the values and, what is the same, the practices, of the dominant classes. The epistemological principle of praxis that applies to all reality has, as we have seen, application to the rereading of canonical writings. No inconsistency can be tolerated here. All militants seek a complete integration of all the different elements of their existence.

At this point a few observations must be attempted in aid of such an integration. José Ramos-Regidor, who is a good analyst of this problem, calls attention to the incompatability of a certain number of contemporary christological formulations with the praxis of class struggle:

The powerless Christ, symbol and leaven of the people's defeat, of human beings crushed by those in power, of submission and resignation, of a fatalistic spirituality based on suffering.

The all-powerful Christ, the heavenly monarch, the religious image of the absolute power of tyrants and their accomplices, the supporter of aristocracies and dictatorships, a symbol of the infallible and ubiquitous state.

The bosom-friend Christ of a private, subjective, and individualistic religiosity, which convinces believers that they can reach personal perfection, "the one thing necessary," no matter what form the state may assume. (This image of Christ acts as a bulwark against all the encroachments of secular society and leads the faithful to be completely unconcerned about the necessary transformation of society.)

Christ as a third force, the great-hearted conciliator of the dominating and the dominated, all members together in a church of different classes with Christ acting as its heart and rallying point.

A Christ at the service of force, a sponsor of fascist ideology, and a proponent of the necessity of taking up arms and adopting a certain number of extraordinary measures to save Christian civilization from the international atheistic communist offensive, although the measures adopted raise doubts about Christian civilization. (This Christ is an ally of Pinochet and the Lebanese Christian militia arrayed against infidel Muslim Palestinians.) Obviously, depending on historical developments in particular milieus, when Christ is used as a reference point, the center of gravity is made to shift from right-center to extreme right.[10] Countertheology is a counterbalance—the criticism and denunciation of traditional formulations.

An attempt will be made here to indicate the dominant traits of a christology of revolutionary praxis, putting together a certain number of characteristics scattered throughout preceding pages. As Fernando Belo has done, emphasis will be placed on the importance of persons with a threefold practice—bodily, social, and historical. Such persons attract others to follow them and at the same time present themselves to them as the source and standard of their own practice. A materialist reading discloses a Jesus who stands up against the order of capitalist exploitation, of foreign oppression, and of religious alienation as represented by the temple; it shows him as a liberator of bodies—that is, of real persons, capable of building up a self-determined communist society administered by adults. His resurrection is the decisive sign and promise that his work, systematically and forcibly attacked by the great ones of this world, opens up to the poor a future life that death can neither diminish nor destroy.

The word of Jesus is creative if only because it makes understandable a dynamic class option, that of the combatants involved in all the struggles in which the future of humankind is being decided today. His word is completely credible because, rejecting all idealistic detachment, he confronts the very core of economic, political, and religious power, and pays with his life for his categorical commitment. When men and women appeal to him and refer to him in their revolutionary praxis, then is the *ecclesia,* the church, or community of the living, as a small comradely cell, contesting the established order and made manifest in history, a harbinger of the just society to come.

In Galatians 3:26–28, Paul develops a utopian vision of the church as a prophetic society freed of the hallowed taboos of race, class, and sex, and dedicated to a practice necessarily subversive of the established order, especially in regard to the status of women. Those who encounter and join this group of "free followers" find that any complicity—internal or external—that they might have had with the enemy is attacked and overcome. A new society and a new human being are born; their appearance involves and proclaims an irreversible event, the birth of a new humanity. With the end of all institutional violence, the reconciliation of oppressed and oppressors will be possible because new relationships, based on equality, will finally be realized.

The countenance of the new humanity is limned more and more clearly and fully by daily praxis as praxis itself becomes better understood and more deeply rooted. And if anybody wants to know the why of this reference, the why of this (endlessly surprising!) encounter: it simply is and it keeps on growing and developing. Militants have no reason to be either apologetic or proud about it; they are and want to be ever more revolutionary and Christian.

Praxis bonded to the living Jesus is the only way to live love, to make love concretely manifest in class struggles, to act effectively to free the enslaved—the dominated *and* their oppressors. The only true solidarity with the latter is to oppose them; it is the only real way to show them love. So let there no longer be contradiction but dialectical complementarity between revolution and conversion; let there no longer be antagonism but fundamental unity between conflict and love. When we refuse to make these paired conditions antithetical, it means that we reject the evasion of being "apolitical," that we show ourselves unwilling to serve as accomplices, objectively, of the dominant classes, and that today we are living a concrete and realistic existence with and for all humankind in history.

Love, indeed, deteriorates into paternalism when it acts only *for* others, and it can be said to be *with* humanity only when it assumes the risks of being "against" the dominant classes. Being truly with the oppressed and against those who victimize them is being *for* all and *with* all. Martin Luther King always strongly emphasized that liberating the poor from the rich liberates the rich from themselves; if it gives the victimized their denied dignity and rights, it brings the powerful down from their thrones and introduces them to the human community. In Giulio Girardi's telling words, love will only be really universal when it is love for a single class[11]—when conflicts between classes are at an end and a whole society of free human beings arises.

This kind of thinking usually makes middle-class Christians smile; yet they are the very ones who keep asking themselves how to bridge the gap between their existential experience and their reading of the gospel. At the same time they continue refusing to recognize that the gap they see is nothing but their own obdurate distancing of themselves from the oppressed.

To experience how the gap can be closed we have only to meet, in some concrete postrevolutionary society, human beings divested of their former privileges attesting, with a certain peace and joy, to their happiness at being from now on "like others"— that is, really *with* others. We have only to hear them testify to their surprise at having been despoiled of what they *had* and thereby restored to what they really *are,* to hear them speak of their relief at having been "reduced"—no, promoted!—to the dignity of the common individual. Now at last they possess and enjoy a sort of immediate and direct capacity for understanding the gospel! Here is a gauge to measure the ultimate challenge of class struggles: the resurrection of human beings condemned and done to death because their social positions cast them in the role of oppressors. Vietnam offers a number of illustrations of the parable of the prodigal son: the son who wants to dominate and to possess becomes a stranger to his brother but returns to life and, from being lost to society, is found and given a share in building the future.

Marxism distinguishes between natural death, the mark of the finiteness of individuals, their unchanging and never-to-be-denied submission to the law of their species, and the violent death forced upon individuals as members of the dominated classes by an economic system and work conditions inflicted upon them by capitalist management. (This is a perspective that personalist idealism too often passes over, largely because of a mistaken reading of the first two chapters of Genesis, which leads one to conclude that the individual precedes society.) As things are, for twenty-four hours out of twenty-four, workers lead an abnormal living death that is a scandal. Not only men and women themselves but also their children are given less consideration than the machines to which the workers are chained and the merchandise that they produce; they are at one and the same time machines and the cheapest, most mishandled products of capitalist society.

From all this we reach the surprising conclusion that the object of revolution is to restore natural death to the oppressed. They have been robbed of it by a capitalist system that has sentenced them to a violent death through structures of exploitation maintained by oppressive power and justified by every agent of an alienating ideology.[12] Who can fail to grasp the paradox that giving natural death back to persons means giving them back real life as it has been written within the parameters of birth and death?

Humanity in the Concrete, the Measure of Theology

We have now reached a point where we meet the inevitable objection made by apolitical idealists and all those who hold to traditional theology: all you are doing is giving Jesus a new label, another guise. What you are imposing on him is just as foreign to him as what you are denouncing. He is precisely the one who eludes *every* label.

It is worthwhile meeting this objection, which once led an old Christian to say to a young nonconformist theologian, "You have done away with my Lord."

Quite some time ago everybody—except for some behind-the-times literalists and illiterates—came to recognize the fact that the only Jesus we know does have a label and does wear a uniform. Traditional theology speaks, and rightly so, of a Matthean, a Marcan, a Lucan, a Johannine, and a Pauline Jesus. A Chalcedonian, Thomistic, and Bultmannian christology are also recognized. Belo goes still further by distinguishing within the same Marcan presentation a theological and a messianic level. And it is worth the trouble to pursue the lines of thought in "heretical" readings—the Marcionite, Arian, and Muntzerian readings—of Jesus. On more than one score, they furnish some interesting correctives to successive "orthodox" interpretations. Furthermore, both groups of works can usefully be submitted to a materialist reading so that their classist nature and role—whether in the service of political and ecclesiastical powers or in opposition to them—are brought to light. This has value when applied to Christian doctrines, community structures, forms of celebration, liturgical texts, and other phenomena. The result is most often sadly obvious: the most forward looking eucharistic prayers seem dated, otherworldly, abstract, and unrelated to the here and now. The concrete human being rooted in history is apparently forgotten in ecclesiastical language. The faithful are introduced "into a schema of relationships between God and humanity that is surely not without guile in its potentiality for contributing to the restoration and functioning of conservative social ideologies."[13] From all appearances, no break of any real magnitude has been made from the days of the "imperial parliamentary" councils.

As existing social relationships are controverted, attenuated, and rejected, the search goes on for new types of social relationships. If Christians are asking for new forms for celebrating the death and resurrection of Christ, are they to receive nothing more than a change of ideological symbols? Militants will have to beware of forgetting that, if the guise in which we apprehend Jesus is inevitably a uniform of some sort, nobody can take him over completely; he is in thrall to no one. Indeed he is the one who takes over his disciples. Yet, at the same time, those who undergo this existential experience are not prevented from apprehending him, from comprehending and expressing him, in their own categories. When Jesus is acknowledged as standing above and beyond the ideologies of domination and of liberation, he is not freed of every mask but simply appears to us with another ideological cover. What difference does that make? Must we have him turn his back on Christians who belong to the system, on religious fascists, on those who refuse to face up to history, on revolutionary militants? We do well to guard against answering that question too quickly and with too much assurance.

Nevertheless, it can be said that when we follow and confess Jesus as one of the poor, we perceive and express him in categories that correspond to the uniform that he chose to wear: according to everything that the Bible has to say, he was identified with the marginated and considered as one of them. He is less miscast in the rags of the poor—for they are not at variance with what he wanted to be—than in the showy clothing of the rich. To live in solidarity with the crucified of our times, is, inevitably, to find Jesus among them. To be actively engaged in realizing a new world and a new humanity, is to be on his side, to share in his way of doing things. It means backing a positive outcome of history as both the fruit of human effort and an unmerited surprise. Never to be a party to defeat and death is to act in companionship with the one who rose from the dead.

In assigning labels—provisional and always to be at the same time avoided and dared—there is a consistency, a congruence, that cuts across all ideologies and comes very close to the living person of Jesus. Sometimes he seems to be within touching distance; in any case, we are constantly being vivified by a life that reaches beyond our own and carries us forward into a history out of our reach.[14]

All this is not to say that the practice of the faith is easier and more natural for militants than for others. What it comes down to for them is a decision taken once and for all and yet to be repeated over and over again; a gift to be received and a daily victory to be won. Measuring the distance between the practice of the Messiah and the practice of his disciples is often a bitter experience. Militants cannot do without forgiveness; it is just as indispensable for them as the daily bread that they ask for in the same breath. This being so, what is an essential element in the practice of Christian revolutionaries leads to the deep joy of constantly validating the consistency of their lives: solidarity with the crucified, shoulder-to-shoulder comradeship with all freedom fighters, membership in the confraternity of all who are serving as midwives of the future!

Pride has no place in all this; nonetheless, militants know that, if they had it to do over again, they would take the same road. And not for anything in the world would they want to change their identity—that is, their practice.

The accusation of "left-wing clericalism" has no substance; first, because any clericalism, whatever its trademark, is "rightist." Besides, when real solidarity exists, roles disappear. Conscientization puts an end to "priest," "master," "father." In a Christian setting, fellowship engenders a church of the people. In the political arena, it gives rise to a society—a social cell— that is socialist and self-managing.

Chapter 6

Families

From the Social to the Personal

The anthropological upheaval brought about by the rupture of the dominant theo-ideology has had considerable repercussions on family thinking and practice. If it is true that any particular, concrete person—a real person—is a social being before becoming conscious of himself or herself as a person, this raises a basic question about the whole line of personalist reasoning, whether humanist or Christian. And, finally, the family ceases to be the primary cell in which a child is developed and socialized. Of course, in the nature of things, a child is born and reared within a family circle, but the family is far from being the chief constituent among all the elements of society. Instead, it is its first product, its local concretization, as diverse as there are areas, epochs, classes, and cultures. Here, as in other instances, the macrosociological unit precedes and determines the microsociological. Because of this, all discussion about *the family* in general is absurd; we can only talk about "families" and, for them to be spoken of sensibly, it is important for them to be reinstated in their respective environments. Marx is unequivocally clear on this point and we can do nothing but admit how sound his critique is—though, at the same time, we cannot help being amazed at his optimism about the bourgeois family—but then he is undoubtedly being more ironic than not in what he says:

On what foundation is the present family, the bourgeois family, based? On capital, on private gain. In its completely developed form this family exists only among the bourgeoisie. But this state of things finds its complement in the practical absence of the family among the proletarians, and in public prostitution. . . .

The bourgeois clap-trap about the family and education, about the hallowed co-relation of parent and child becomes all the more disgusting the more, by the action of modern industry, all family ties among the proletarians are torn asunder and their children transformed into simple articles of commerce and instruments of labor.[1]

It will be said that this is an outdated statement, that agricultural and industrial workers were integrated into consumer society long ago and have become members of the lower middle class. Really? Was it not early in 1977 that Raymond Barre, the French prime minister, was calmly talking about "mobile employment" as a remedy for unemployment? The miserable circumstances of foreign workers, separated for months and years from their wives and children, and the emotional and sexual anguish this entails, is passed over in racist discussions about the potential menace posed for society in the latent aggressiveness of these tanned men from the south. Yet their lot bids fair to become the fate of all those in the labor market who cannot find takers. A great deal of lamentation about it goes on—like the feeble regrets voiced about the battalions of official and unofficial prostitutes—but nothing is done to attack the cause: the existence of a society in which the only real imperatives are maximizing profits in order to maximize power, or maximizing power in order to maximize profits.

Yet the dominant moral theology pursues its abstract and unruffled course, doing nothing to pose a threat to the established order: humanity is a personal being. It is understood, of course, that it cannot be reduced to an individual—and one of our leading moral philosophers unsmilingly makes the statement that a celibate is not a whole person! Personalist humanism is relational: it addresses itself to neighbor, love of the other, the gift and sacrifice that characterize an authentic life. Among "neighbors," the closest one, "the alter ego," is the partner in a monogamous couple, the basic cell of every sound society, which the churches and the civil laws have the duty to promote and protect. In the best of cases, the primary function of sexuality is to express the unity of the couple and the uniqueness of their loving relationship. Nonetheless, sexuality also serves the ends of the Master of history who, through love, continues his work of creative love. Children, the fruit, if not the end of conjugal love, are to take over for their parents. They are, together with the couple's professional activity, the link with society in all its close and distant dimensions. A person's activity moves out in expanding circles from neighbor to associate, from the intimate relationships of *agape* to the more remote relations directed to justice.

In a work that has played an important role in awakening political consciousness among Protestant youth groups, Paul Ricoeur has developed the broad lines of this theme from another perspective:

> We are not living, I am tempted to say, in a neighborly world but in a world of the "socius." A socius is the one whom I come in touch with, relate to mediately, through his or her social function; I come in touch with him or her "insofar as". . . . As soon as I reduce the theology of neighbor to a theology of encounter, I lose the fundamental significance of God's lordship over *history*. . . . That is what a "reactionary" interpretation of the relationships of socius and of neighbor fails to encompass; as soon as the theme of neighbor is cut away from the social context in which it makes its impact on history, it quickly turns into sterile regret and falls prey to a terrible appetite for some sort of avenging catastrophe. . . . On the other hand, it must be said that it is history, and its dialectic of neighbor and socius, that preserves the *breadth* of charity; yet, ultimately, charity governs the relationship of socius and neighbor, giving them a common *intention*. For the theology of charity could not have less extension than the theology of history.[2]

If a warning against every sort of dehumanizing anonymity in regard to "distant" relationships is tragically needed, one against converting love into a private and personal matter is dramatically urgent. By inverting the traditional religious discourse, Ricoeur puts things in their true relationship: the social is primary, and the personal has its place and greatest significance within the social cadre. It can become the heart and the light of the collectivity on the express condition that the distinctive character and the specific constitution of the latter are recognized. Without that, all that is left to us is an individualistic and mystifying idealism.

Yet the habit of speaking of humanity in general, of its nature, of its relationship to God, and of its relational extensions adheres like a barnacle to traditional theology.

When the Protestant Federation of France undertook in 1974 to publish a document on sexuality—relatively progressive, moreover, in some of its approaches—the twenty persons commissioned with its redaction were of one mind in following a schema having nothing to do with the dialectic of socius and neighbor:

> Man and woman (the Bible and human relationships, the goodness of sexuality, the choice of marriage, the choice of celibacy); children (the freedom of procreation, education, adolescence); difficulties, failures, new beginnings (divorce, widowhood, abortion, adoption, norms and anomalies of sexuality); sexual education (role of the family, of the school, of society); conclusion (sexuality and love); some passages of the Bible on sexuality.

This sequence is in itself eloquent. In fact, the whole text, with its apparently biblical timelessness, falls in line—if not in detail at least in its overall perspective—with the dominant ideology and the theology that ideology has standardized and as both of these are reflected in the middle classes that make up the majority of the Protestant population and its leaders during the closing years of the twentieth century. It is all the more interesting and revealing because three years earlier, the same Protestant Federation proclaimed that "In the eyes of the gospel . . . French society today is unacceptable."

Yet, in 1974, it carefully avoided, and not for the first time, posing the question of how this unacceptability is reflected in the sexual thinking and practice of bourgeois Protestants. There is, therefore, something at once bland and bold in the title "Sexuality: A Christian Reflection."[3]

That subject touches on the real family as it has been produced by Western society and as it is reflected in morals claiming to be Christian. It is a microorganism as closed as it is standardized, with unbelievable pretensions of being universal. It possesses a whole arsenal of principles that, for generations of Christians, have served to paralyze every creative impulse and ability: "People don't do that. One doesn't read that. Don't touch that." All this is light years away from St. Augustine's "Love; then do what you will." It makes understandable Gide's wild cry "Families, I hate you!" It sounds like an echo, and doubtless not a fortuitous one, of the gospel passage, "If any man comes to me without hating his father, mother, wife, children, brothers, sisters, yes and his own life too, he cannot be my disciple" (Luke 14:26). The translators of the Common *Bible* thought it necessary to tone down this terrible prouncement. Yet it points out how a family, any family in any society, can be a snare: it can so entrap its members that if one of them severs connections with it in response to an astonishing summons to a new practice of sharing, of opening closed doors, of breaking with the received ideology . . . he or she will be repulsed.

Cellular Egoism

Have no doubt of it, the "Christian family"—or what is commonly understood by that expression—represents, in the overwhelming majority of cases, a devastating of sociological, psychological, and spiritual immobility and blockage. It is a deadend where "political beings" are made impotent and reduced to the state of maimed and tamed individuals, deprived indeed of all that makes any man or woman a responsible citizen of the world. Of course, remarkable exceptions and brilliant successes occur; but the majority of families, so highly praised in religious spheres and tearfully mourned because they are disintegrating, are, more than anything else, places where values and reactions consonant with the established order have been and still are transmitted: ancestor worship, inheritance, ideological continuity, obsequious respect for social advancement and professional success, and the acquisition of wealth.

Who has not become aware that being brought up on the ideal, "Be a leader!" and the injunction, "You have to be first in everything!"—which is somehow not incompatible with the commandment to love one's neighbor—prepares a person with everything needed to develop a fascist character and fascist conduct? Families are undoubtedly reproductive cells . . . but first and always, of ideas about the world and structures that correspond with maintaining the socio-political status quo! As André Burguière has written:

> The question arises whether a person kept in such prolonged dependence upon a mother and a parental group does not become a hyperfamilial animal, incapable of conceiving of any other social tie save as a dim projection of the parental bond: a need to be on familiar terms with others, to fraternize. And a need to find in patron, king, president, or leader, a castigating father or a scolding mother.[4]

The winning trump in these social hierarchies—including the ecclesiastical—is the effective and frightful cellular egoism. It dominates the whole life of families and finds its perfect symbol in the urban habitat and the cellular construction to be found in the "better" housing: in detached homes in comfortable suburbs; in fine apartments in restricted metropolitan areas. All are so many island fortresses where residents take refuge from indiscreet eyes, in calculated ignorance of associates, of course, but also of neighbors. In heavily populated areas, the dominant ideology is largely responsible for the lack of collective awareness. Residents defend themselves from any loud proximity of others, from mixing with just anyone, protecting what they believe to be their privacy but what is often nothing but a rejection of others.

Even the workers' quarters do not escape being atomized, a process that leaves their families defenseless against the interests that are exploiting them. The ridiculously small number of workers who are members of consumer cooperatives, of neighborhood associations, and of committees to combat noise, industrial pollution, and speculation in real estate obviously plays into the hands of their families' worst enemies.

No doubt, *inside* "the islands" residents do practice altruistic virtues of solidarity and sacrifice; no doubt, too, confrontations take place that can assume the character of muted hatred, particularly between husband and wife, each seeking compensation for their social failures, but these are carried on behind a facade, for one must not compromise the social roles and chances of familiar enemies. Be that as it may, middle-class families, including those that are Christian, comprise a species of self-sufficient and xenophobic tumor, thanks to the closed border between families and the outside world. If that frontier is not actually impenetrable, it is intended to be. Its guardians are manifold: rites, myths, key words, conformity to type, a feeling of superiority, moral principles, and religious practices. These families form a collectivity, but are unaware of it. Provincial traditions enable them to hold off "the other," the stranger, the unexpected, anything from the outside that could move or surprise or arouse them to participate in common action. Everything is done to serve the cell itself, to promote its distinguished image, its respectability, and its material interests, the whole purpose of the enterprise demanding an incredible expenditure of energy and unremitting attention.

In his study *La paroisse, communauté eucharistique*,[5] Casiano Floristán analyzes the transition of Christianity from a movement of eschatological hope and liberation to a personal and private matter. In its beginnings the Christian community or *paroikia* was a fresh new creation, open and receptive; it centered around a common project directed *beyond* its own circle—the proclamation of the gospel to persons of every category: rich and poor, learned and ignorant, enslaved and free, men and women, especially those whom the pagan world despised and rejected. As the etymology of the term (*paroikia*, "house of a stranger") suggests, the Christian community was completely caught up in and directed to the great urban metropolis and its hundreds of thousands of inhabitants. In regard to the city and its inhabitants, it was conscious of being in complete solidarity with them and, at one and the same time, entirely foreign. In relation to the dominant ideologies and practices it was a new, original group, and yet it held out to the masses both promise and future. In its diversity it was present to a heterogeneous city. It lived in an astonishing balance of innovation and tradition, of shared responsibilities and communal autonomy. Generally speaking, this is what the evidence tells us, in spite of some initiatives that came to grief and some that achieved only mediocrity.

During the third and fourth centuries, particularly in Gaul, and, subsequently, during the age of the barbarian invasions, the community took root in the countryside and allowed itself to become entangled in the local religion, in more or less syncretic religious practices that attributed a sacred character to places and to natural phenomena. It was progressively infiltrated by the unchanging traditions and traditional virtues of the rural masses. The city cell, eschatological and wide open, was increasingly taken over and standardized by fugitives in the rural exodus—diehards, standpatters, insulars. The small commando units of foreigners and travelers came to an end, overcome and assimilated by the formidable weight of a milieu as closed as it was immovable. The ecclesiastical building became the center of the city; the priest or bishop became its leader. A bourgeois ideology grounded in peasant virtues and persistence, nostalgic for an idealized past, sentimental and self-seeking, took over. The social order was more and more dominated by an institution that offered no real openness or challenge and, in general, was not slow to identify "christianized" society with the kingdom announced by Jesus. The German language gives an excellent example of the overlapping of the social and the religious: the word *Gemeinde* stands for both the civil commune and the religious community.

Alfred Loisy's witticism is well known: "Jesus announced the kingdom of God, but it was the church that came." A calm observation can be added: by his practice Jesus inaugurated the venture of a new humanity. But after the original exodus what remained was the parish, composed of secluded families living side by side. Surely putting the gospel into practice consists not in achieving success but in making a breakthrough, not in getting established but in pressing forward, not in acquiring security but in taking risks.

Attempts at communitarian reform have failed in uncounted numbers, stifled by an immovable Christian family and its refusal to allow itself to be moved an inch beyond its settled convictions and unshakable prejudices. Efforts to introduce liturgical or catechetical innovations, to put into effect some freedom and ease in the relationships among its members, to implement a renewal of sacramental practices, have all run up against an awesome inertia. A little group of Christians on the move find themselves isolated and sometimes beset by the growing distrust of the majority, who suspect that the true religion is somehow being tampered with—"You are changing our religion on us!" A wave of traditionalist protest arises, a direct expression of family myths and rites. These consist essentially in "rites of passage": birth, puberty, marriage, and death—blessing them, so to speak; protecting life as an absolute value; transforming the gospel into life insurance and Jesus into one of the numerous manifestations of the Phoenician god Baal, an idol of fecundity and success. A message of exodus and liberation, of death and resurrection, cannot be reduced, with impunity, to the natural cycles of the seasons, of sowing and harvesting, of saving and investing, of reaping and receiving dividends, or to the continual renewal of the human community by the succession of generations through birth and death.

"We have just moved into our house, Father," said a woman of the Cévennes region, in justification for her request to have a baptism at home, contrary to the rule specifying that it should be performed during the Sunday service. "If a single drop of water falls on the floor, that will do for the whole house."⁶ This magical naturalization of Christianity spells death to the gospel. We need go no further to find an explanation for the present mushrooming of interest in religion and the crisis of uncertainty and confusion taking place in every ecclesiastical institution.

The Rite of Spring (Stravinsky-Cohn Bendit)

If we suppress what ought to be spread abroad, if we continually silence the song birds and tolerate without any reaction the extinction of the Spirit, the gospel will be revealed elsewhere. Where a conformist religion has imprisoned it, militancy has, as we have seen, given it freedom. Certain events trigger an unpreventable explosion; a tremendous demonstration against all the perversions that have disfigured the gospel suddenly erupts. That is what occurred in May 1968 when a festive revolt of university students took place in Paris; a closed world suddenly burst open under the pressure of a tidal wave as unexpected as it was irresistible. Words, the overabundant verbiage of the dominant ideology, were taken over—an occurrence a hundred times more important than the taking of the empty Bastille, a ridiculous symbol of the divine right of power. At one stroke, a blaze of communication flared up. Those who experienced it will never forget it; something more than the barricades and parades, something more than the complex ploys and maneuvers of those in power, it had an extraordinary character and significance. What uplifted the heart with joy was the coming together, the sharing, the overturning of barriers that had separated people of different ages and milieus, the talking together, the challenging, the listening, the explaining. All at once, the Sorbonne, the Odéon, the Boulevard Saint-Michel were restored to their primary purpose: from being encumbered by traffic and glutted with magisterial oratory, they were won back by creative conversation. The young greeted each other as brothers and sisters, booed each other as adversaries, discovered each other as comrades; every acquaintance became a neighbor. A foolish—or realistic—utopia burst the bonds of customary ways of acting and speaking. Dreamers dreamed dreams, discovering that until then they had been living through a nightmare. It was like the morning of the seventh day, the dawn of a cosmic Easter, the ninth hour of a still unnamed and unnamable Pentecost. Graffiti announced:

—Death is of necessity a counterrevolution.
—We refuse to accept a world where you have to choose between dying of hunger or perishing of boredom.
—Forward, comrade, the old world lies behind you.[7]

How frightened the Establishment was!—all those who suddenly felt the absolute vertigo of their whole mental world tottering: their accepted ideas, their titles, their paternal, professional, patronal, and pastoral authorities radically devaluated; their systems bankrupted; their calculations set at naught; their

reason for being, that is—rather, the unreason for their possessing—in complete dissolution. Then they began to cry subversion
and revolution, to run for refuge to their Baden-Badens and Col-
ombeys, packing their suitcases and preparing to change sides.
They waited for gasoline to be available again, for the end of the
railroad strike, for the next speech of General de Gaulle, completely bewildered by the loss of their functions and social roles
and by the discovery of their complete lack of intellectual, moral,
and religious credibility. They shouted to the heavens for help and
shamefully greeted the mobile police units as angels responding to
their anguished prayers, earthly messengers of their gods of Order, Hierarchy, and Merit. They were incapable of seeing or
hearing or experiencing any joy, entirely preoccupied as they were
with dashing for their back-up shelters and securities. Masochis-
tic mourners joined in guarding a dead hope; they lost their heads
like the women who once discovered an empty tomb. And what
were they to do? Let them turn to the "bible" of the witnesses and
makers of the revolt; many of its (graffiti) verses echo the great
hope of prophets and apostles:

　　—To cry out against death is to call for life.
　　—Life may not be beautiful; but compared to survival, it
has its charms.
　　—Ten days of happiness already.
　　—Be realists; demand the impossible.[8]

All the liturgies scrupulously reproduced in traditionalist celebrations or timidly arranged by progressive groups exploded in
the streets in a festival of persons on the move, knowing full well
that they were not going to transform the world, not even French
society, but resolved that, while they waited for what they themselves could not effect, they would live a few weeks that would be
written on their calendars and in their hearts for lifetime remembrance.

To be sure, we have yet to make our way through some dark
tunnels. The Czechoslovakian people especially have a long hard
journey ahead. It went through the same experience that we did,
acting in a completely reasonable and politically responsible man-
ner, and have since been plunged into the depths of an endless

night. Yet the memory of a world springtime, of a festival of freedom, of a celebration of foolish liberality, continues to foster hope, the rejection of the intolerable, and the wager that persons will not always resign themselves to being confined to either ideological or police lockups. The revolt of the whole person to challenge the meaning of life will end by bursting the bolts and bars of capitalist and bureaucratic systems:

—I decree a state of unending good times.

—My thinking is not revolutionary if it does not involve revolutionary action in educational, familial, political, and amorous groups.

—Freedom is the right to silence.

—Take a look at your work, the emptiness and torment of it.

—The one pleasure of the bourgeoisie is to debase everyone.[9]

On April 22, 1977, in a televised dialogue with Maurice Grimaud, who was the prefect of police in 1968, Daniel Cohn Bendit exclaimed: "The scuffle was not important; what was important was the way everyone got together, embraced each other. . . ." But the bourgeois order was so frightened by what it perceived as subversive in these new personal relationships, in these embraces between militants, that it interpreted these expressions of a tremendous desire for living as paving stones flung at the shields of order. Or, rather, having dealt blows to words freely spoken and love freely given, they were hypocritically scandalized at having the stones that they themselves had cast thrown back at them!

—Teachers, you are as old as your culture; your modernism amounts to nothing but the updating of the police.

—Thinking is not revolutionary; action is what revolution is all about.

—From solitariness to solidarity at last.

—Speaking for whom? How do we get from talking to doing?

—Violate your Alma Mater.

—What is a teacher, a god? Both are father images and, by definition, fulfill an oppressive function.

—Before dying for an ideal, don't make your last will; beget a child worthy of its father.

—Instead of a father given to talk, a son committed to action.[10]

Evidently this talk of breaking away was an unpardonable act of defiance and would have to be quashed by every means—stick, carrot, and calumny—used by turns or all at the same time. And this in spite of the analysis made by others foreign, if not unfriendly, to the celebration:

The students rejected a university with just one mission—to adapt them to society today. . . . The students were upset at the idea of a world that would not offer them employment and would look upon their diplomas, so dearly acquired, as of little worth. In demanding autonomy and self-management of the university, the students were intentionally attacking technocratic society . . . where persons are identified with their functions, where they have no other future than playing the game of climbing the social ladder and reaching their prefabricated place inside a "box."[11]

Or again:

It was a liturgy of being, an explosive *festival* that trespassed upon the preserves of day-to-day dullness . . . a festival of coming together and sharing, with barricades marking off a sacred space where a miracle seemed possible at any moment. . . .

They had the intuition of a pan-human, global consciousness in the making, urging, at the same time, the constant and creative affirmation of the unique character of each person. A socialist tradition and an anarchist tradition expressed in well-organized language indicate, by the fact of their convergence and the impossibility of their integration, the two dimensions of human communion: the unity of humankind and the uniqueness of every human being.[12]

In these two quotations, the authors refer to the past with relief; for them it is over and done, a matter of history, even if a "spiritual crisis" in need of remedy remains in evidence. The great tradition about the family and its natural extensions— schools, universities, churches—leads no further than to a pious reflection on the need to tidy up the traditional message and to experience a creative outpouring of the Holy Spirit. It could and should have been concerned with something quite different: if a whole generation of privileged youth, those to whom capitalist society has given access to the university so that they may become the cadres of a society for tomorrow that will be homogeneous with that of today, if, together with them, sociologists and lead- ing analysts of collective pathologies reject the world of domesti- cative education in which they grew up from childhood, surely that is primarily because they see nothing ahead of them except intellectual unemployment. Yet there is another reason as well: the students refused to be the running dogs charged with rounding up and neutralizing the exploited masses. Finally, they have dis- covered the innovative character of the future in comparison with the present and the past. In economic, socio-political, and ideo- logical areas, their rejection expresses the birth of a revolutionary consciousness and militancy—which does not mean that every- thing is going to change with this generation but that we have entered into a new stage of Western history and nothing will ever be the same again.

A School for Fathers

To make a gospel reading of this by no means outdated event demands a very concrete comprehension of the verses about the angel's annunciation to Zacharias. According to the text of the third evangelist, the ministry of John the Baptist will be to ". . . bring back many of the sons of Israel to the Lord their God. With the power and spirit of Elijah, he will go before him *to turn the hearts of fathers toward their children* and the disobedient back to the wisdom that the virtuous have, preparing for the Lord a people fit for him" (Luke 1:16-17). The central statement of the passage is an abbreviated quotation from Malachi 3:23-24. The last of the Old Testament prophets announces the second coming of Elijah, identified in the New Testament as John the Baptist: "Know that I am going to send you Elijah the prophet before my day comes, that great and terrible day. He shall turn the hearts of the fathers toward their children and the hearts of the children toward their fathers. . . ."

The reciprocity centered in the Old Testament text forms a sort of circle entirely missing from the New Testament quotation, where there is no question of mutual give-and-take, where the picture is not of a balanced community, with each generation attentive to the other and prepared to learn from it, doing everything on its part to maintain unity. The New Testament has its face turned to the future, looking to a time ahead challenging and expanding the present, a time characteristic of the new economy inaugurated by the precursor of Jesus. Fathers are urged to be converted to their children, the old to the young, the past to the morrow. In this way they will be true offspring of Israel, true Israelites according to the spirit and not just according to the flesh; in this way they will become the disobedient returning to the wisdom of the virtuous, brought back to the Lord their God as "a people made fit for him."

The challenge is tremendous and the question put to allegedly Christian families is radical. Everything is geared to retain their hold on their children, to bring them up in the ancestral virtues, traditions, and patrimonies, to protect and to condition them, forming them in accordance with the interests and ideals of the generation holding power in society and in the family. And it is well that parents rather than grandparents have the last word, though grandparents are often capable of remarkable understanding and support.

We do well not to underestimate the truth in Tucholsky's sarcasm:

> We are very close to one another. A stranger would never be permitted to get as close to you as the cousin of your sister-in-law on the claim of being related to you. . . . Did not the ancient Greeks call their close kin the most beloved of all? The present generation of youth calls them something else, and has it in for the family even more. Later on they themselves will be founding families resembling on every point those that preceded them . . . and if the whole world were to come to an end, the fear is that in the hereafter an angel

might come to meet you, softly fluttering a fan of feathers:
"Tell me, aren't we related?" Flustered, pierced to your
heart's core, you will precipitate your flight—toward hell.
But it will do you no good. Because that is where they all are,
all the others.[13]

Something tragic happened to Christianity centuries ago and is
still at work. Did it not come about by baptizing—and continuing
to baptize—the structure of the Jewish family, by reducing it to its
central core, parents and children, with a nebula of close and distant kin and, more than anything else, by placing its center of
gravity in the past and by hallowing natural continuity, the biological process, with baptism, confirmation, and marriage? For
the Old Testament to do this made good sense: its foundations
rested upon continuity, tradition, genealogy—with male circum-
cision as its automatic insignia—because the Messiah was to be
born in that biologico-spiritual family. Every father and every
mother expecting a child could hope that it would be the one for
whom the whole world was waiting. The family cell and the transmission of the promise were of greater importance than the transmission of life itself. Not only was it necessary to have children
(and a misfortune not to have them—Sarah, Anne, and Elizabeth
were afflicted women until a miracle made them mothers), but to
have children by any means (which is the reason for the "scan-
dalous" stories of the Old Testament from Tamar through Rahab
the prostitute to Ruth, and it mattered little that these women
were pagans as long as they gave birth to sons of the covenant).
However, these children did have to be brought up in the faith of
their forebears, for what constituted Israel was the paradox of
both a natural line and fidelity to long-standing expectations, to
the promise received, to the spirituality of the patriarchs Abraham, Isaac, and Jacob.

In the New Testament, things are different; the coming of Jesus
did away with the alienating structures that recognized and supported only what renewed the past. The one whom the world had
been waiting for had come and the community that he gathered
together did not depend in any way upon natural generation. It
was constituted by the intervention of the Spirit in the lives of

adults, whatever their origin, race, language, nation, or family might be. This was understood at least by the first generation, but those who followed were not slow to fall back into sacralizing marital sexuality, to the fecundity of the married couple, to the family cell offering every guarantee for the "natural" reproduction of Christian values. The Old Testament was concerned for the most part with the continuity of a spiritual history through the begetting of generations, whereas the New Testament placed its emphasis on the newness of what was to come, on the unexpected filiations that would come about when and where God so willed.

Children, who are not the end but only the possible and not the obligatory consequence of the union of man and woman, are not automatically a prolongation of what their parents have been. And if all of us are at the same time jealous of the young (who, just by existing, remind us adults of our death) and if we are always inclined to invest our own desire for immortality in them so that when we are no longer on the scene something of us will remain, this must not obscure the fact that every child represents the emergence of someone wholly other. An apparition of the future, the child relegates the generation before it to the past and rolls back the curtain of the future on a world that is new but neither engendered by history nor foreign to it, linked to the passage of time by an originative dialectic of continuity and rupture. The child is not primarily a reproduction of a parental model but a new venture, a unique and irreplaceable being who breaks through the known to open a way to the improbable. This is why the death of a child is a scandal that sends the parents back into the past, back to the known, the usual. For them the future dies, time closes up, life loses meaning. Faced with the death of a child, Camus offers us not an answer or an explanation but the possibility of behaving more rationally than emotionally before the intolerable:

> A yet more noteworthy change was that instead of saying "you" he (the priest) said "we". . . .
> He would keep faith with that great symbol of suffering, the tortured body on the cross; he would stand fast, his back to the wall, and face honestly the terrible problem of a

child's agony. And he would boldly say to those who listened to his words today: "My brothers, a time of testing has come for us all. We must believe everything or deny everything. And who among you, I ask, would dare to deny everything?"[14]

The turning of fathers' hearts toward their children means the greatest possible disinterestedness, a radical divestiture, death to every role and privilege and, so too, entrance to a new life. If, as Paulo Freire has pointed out, all education is in the first place taming and domesticating because it confounds power with authority, because it turns age, ownership, and experience to good account in order to assume the right to condition and contaminate another human being, then the revolt of this person against an abusive pedagogy can be, for him or her as well as for the parents, a liberating Easter, a death to situations and roles of domination and submission and an entrance into the freedom of listening and sharing, teaching and being taught.

The pure marvel of May 1968 can keep on happening: the old can be released from senility; it is possible for them to take a second and a third breath, to become adaptable again, to experience unhoped-for openness of mind and heart, to know the joy of being drawn into action again by an infectious youthfulness, daring, and impudence. All this would mean to experience the truth of a "classless society" as the apostle Paul foretold it: the profanation and destruction of all taboos—classist, cultural, sexual, genealogical, and gerontocratic. Only when woman achieves equality in altereity will we have the beginning of a new world. Is it surprising that today we recognize, almost at a glance, in those who burn with the fire of practice and of the word, a reflection and continuation of the Pentecostal flame? All at once, on May 22, it blazed up in the crowds who went swinging up the Boulevard Saint-Michel shouting, "We are all German Jews!" (And on November 16, 1977: "all lawyers!")

Praxis and Family

The Christian West, a gloomy and conservative family, drags itself along, burdened with moribund traditions and deteriorating structures. It is characterized by retail outlets crammed with non-essential consumer items, sealed-off families, pillage of the Third World and ideological murder of innocents, material wealth and interior poverty, ailing states and meaningless liturgies. Everywhere persons try to keep alive the remains of past glories; they speak the language of yesterday and dream of a time of triumph, ease, and cheer that never existed. The energy invested in collective and private enterprises becomes more and more absurd as checks and reverses mount up. . . . We see persons grow old while denying the advent of a new day; they back into the future, as it were, shedding tears because their children are not realizing the hopes that they themselves failed to fulfill, doing their utmost to preserve, by clinging to immortal principles, family edifices long past any hope of repair. Some, despairing of everything, drag themselves along, looking forward, in anguish and longing, to death.

Anybody can become a child. Becoming a child is a gospel paradox and an expression of true revolutionary militancy; it means having a really ecumenical consciousness, one with global dimensions, one freshened by an untempered and healthy wind blowing from the ends of the earth, quickening the confined lives of individuals and sweeping the fog from their perspectives. Nothing else can give us all direction and the will to live, the capacity to be adaptable and creative. Recapturing youth is linked with the death of personal ambitions. They, like cholesterol in the arteries, damage the hearts of men and women and age them prematurely.

Praxis contravenes everything that bears the disfiguring traits of wealth—racism, fascism, and the spirit of domination; it makes nothing of the assets and honor of the bourgeois family, does away with its prejudices and standoffishness, its pride, its urge to maintain and defend its distinctive image.

Militants know themselves to be directed to other, more realistic, ends. And they have nothing but contempt for all the pseudo values that serve as alibis for having nothing to do with common interests, interdependent responsibilities, and historical tasks. Breaking away from the dominant classes and their ideological poison gives the lives of liberation fighters a lightness, a responsiveness, an openness that, far from weakening with age, keep flourishing and deepening as long as they are true to themselves and keep moving ahead even when they seem at times defeated. Today the witnessing done by the martyr countries in the southern cone of Latin America depends upon their deep roots in popular awareness and action. As the examples of Portugal and Spain clearly show, a half century and more of implacable oppression cannot break the revolutionary spirit of a people. The greatest danger that it has to fear is neither dictatorship nor torture but, while escaping those, becoming bogged down in the intermeshings of so-called social democratic politics.

Families are powerful forces for neutralizing energies and destroying vocations that are not in conformity with accepted and, in a sense, canonical models. Yet with a change of perspective, they can regain their health and a social role. In 1977 a young German paralyzed by the moral and police order of the Federal Republic of Germany, a second-string imperialism in the service of "national security," wrote:

> When I think of my country and numerous exchanges taking place among the young who are seeking a communion that would make life possible, I believe that I can say that the vision of humankind as just one family is absolutely essential and indeed provocative. . . . The characteristic isolation of our society, an isolation that engenders fear, will then be breached at some points. And the fear of losing our security when we say no to a university or to some enterprise and become thereby a sign of contradiction will diminish.[15]

For families, the Copernican revolution consists in abandoning the idea that the whole world is an extension of that basic cell and exists to serve its ends. It means learning to think of and to live marriage, celibacy, the masculine-feminine dialectic, parent-child relationships, the professions, and community life within and for the good of the whole social enterprise. Unconsciously, bourgeois families want to do this; if they become aware of an imperative social alternative, they can be cured of their mortal illness—an infarcted mentality. It, as Tucholsky pointedly remarks, survives through years of adolescent crisis and is discovered intact in the lives of young adults who believe themselves to be independent.

To look at it in another way—what will break open family circles, vicious circles where promiscuousness and loneliness, disguised egoism and suppressed violence, boredom and fugitive dreams of escape convolve, is the social praxis created by a new society.

Collectivity and the Future

We must not have any illusions, however. Among alienations of every kind, the alienation linked with the ideology of the dominant family is the most tenacious, and few revolutions have succeeded in shaking off its yoke, although Cuba and Vietnam perhaps have done so. Contrary to the line of thought popular in milieus that tend to denounce the present time as degraded—the better to brake any movement toward the future—the most credible research and statistical studies confirm the formidable resistance of the family prison.

Today families are more durable than in the past because of progress in medicine; they are more closed because of their concentration in the nuclear family; they are more untouchable because they are everywhere presented as the refuge from a hostile world over which we have no control; they are more united because they have a living (electronic) ikon, the television set, with its daily diffusion of poisonous publicity promoting materialist consumerism. Schools take their cue from the family; instead of pursuing an approach open to political life, they take the family as their basis so that society, as it is, may keep on being reproduced. They make children into reflections of their parents instead of encouraging parents to become students of their children:

> The family has never been stronger! It is or seems to be the last refuge for the affective values stripped from daily life, a small island of peace in war, the only garden where someone can venture the risky business of celebrating Love and Happiness. A frightening project, an ambition beyond bounds. The small bourgeois family, called "the nuclear family" by sociologists, is no longer a community grounded in a larger community. It is an atom among atoms, like the polyps ranged side by side on a coral reef. Take a look at the family that is entrusted with making us happy—ourselves who are

over and over again denied so much we hope for! It is expected to provide love, sensual satisfaction, integral communion, self-discipline, and eternity. In a word, the Absolute. Our laws and institutions, which essay to set themselves up as those of a "progressive liberal democracy"—in plain language, of neocapitalism—attempt to strengthen the image of a family that is the issue of the patriarchal tradition of the countryside allied with an industrial age deformed by its own exigencies. It is therefore, of necessity, a mongrel. A difficult undertaking. . . . Adaptability, yes, but together with stability. The reigning ethic throws some things overboard to keep the watertight family cargo safe.[16]

Happy exceptions exist, and it would be both small-minded and foolish to overlook them. But they close nobody's eyes to the family blind alleys all around us and to the reality hidden by some so-called successes. All the evidence clearly suggests that pathological chains fetter children to parents, parents to children, both unable to sever the umbilical cord—the children incapable of leaving the nest, the parents still brooding over progeny baptized and vaccinated long ago. No doubt exists that, generally speaking, a reciprocal sterilization takes place, both children and parents becoming unproductive, immobile.

The worst cases are those couples who are still young and no longer have anything to say to each other or any reason to keep on living since their "little ones" have left them and they find that they are "all by themselves." What could be a third stage of love, a wonderful time to be together, a period fully enriched by thirty years of shared struggles, joys, and sorrows is often only a desert where a lackluster man and a faded woman, alone and lonely, grope warily around, offering each other so little support that they often see divorce as the only way out of their personal hell. How different that could be if, from the beginning of their close relationship, they had made it a part of a collective undertaking, supported and enlarged by more distant relationships assumed all throughout a militant existence too full for the successive stages of life to exhaust.

Of course, that would not solve every problem; the genetic anomalies, the illnesses, accidents, and deaths that continue to impair and truncate so many lives must be faced. And it is still true that a social being is a person with affectivity, with a hunger for intimacy and privacy. Young children do need the basic cell represented by the couple; but all too quickly a natural dimension of every existence runs the risk of becoming a prison, an opaque matrix where a circumscribed life becomes stifled and stunted. When a larger group can provide a place of apprenticeship for meeting and forming fellowship with others, members of a nuclear family who regard that neighbor-at-a-distance with ignorance or contempt are destructive of their own humanity. What positive energy could be released if the core of this self-sufficient atom could split up under the repeated bombardments of the risks and urgencies of a praxis engendered by either the hope or the realization of new economic and political structures! On the other hand, what an explosion could take place if the atom splitting were done outside an environment capable of channeling it. It is understandable that most regimes resulting from socialist revolutions have drawn back before the terrifying risks of the social disintegration that this would represent.

We can expect, then, that human communities and couples will always continue to be the normal loci for expressions of love and for privileged sexual relations. These families, not necessarily monogamous or consecrated by religion, are the framework for the early years of children's lives, but the well-being of both children and families—multiform associations with a plurality of pedagogies and lifestyles—can be had only through their conscious insertion into the movement of humanity toward the liberation and fulfillment of history. Indeed the priority is situated precisely there: every "sexual revolution" that is not a part of an integral revolutionary undertaking is a waste of energy; at best, it is an extension of that indivisible core, the nuclear family, and stands for only a slight broadening of conjugal-parental egoism. Its social inefficacy is fundamentally counterrevolutionary.

After 1968, nothing so gladdened the hearts of the architects of order as the blow dealt to disenchanted youth by the derailment of a great festival into a hippy movement with its worthless interests—drugs, sexual anarchy, charismatic religiosity—escape mechanisms devoutly desired and strongly encouraged by the powers that be. And the churches are showing a heightened interest in these fringe groups: their rebellion in no way calls the system into question. At the same time, redoubled proddings by croziers are being dealt militants in order to retire them from the field.

Militant Christians, to the extent to which their praxis is integrated within a global enterprise, are rediscovering the true import of the family "cell" as the gospel brings it to light; it is and can be no more than *an instrument* in the service of the "recapitulation" of all humankind. Long ago Abraham received a son *only* that he might become a blessing for all the tribes of the earth (Gen. 12:3); he was singled out and made the bearer of the promise only that he might be "the light of nations" and that "all the families of nations" will one day bow down before the liberator of the world (Ps. 22:27; 96:3–13). According to the author of the Letter to the Ephesians, Christ, by entering into the arena with us and taking a real and disinterested part in our struggles, was to destroy "every wall of separation" among us—beginning with the wall between the biologico-spiritual Jewish family and the mass of pagans. Thus in the heart of world history, he became peace, a new space, a new dynamic among separated human beings, categorized as those who are "so far apart" and those who are "very close." He made all of us, even "aliens and foreign visitors," citizens "like all the saints" (the patriarchs, kings, and prophets of the Old Testament) and "part of God's household" (Eph. 2: 13, 19–20). Furthermore, every family, whether natural or spiritual, has its origin in God (Eph. 3:14); God is the source of its existence and the measure of its authenticity. This being so, it is obviously not surprising that, in all the fundamentally antiparticularist legislation of the Old Testament, the decisive test for the authentic character of a family was the way it received the foreigner and the immigrant:

> If a stranger lives with you in your land, do not molest him. You must count him as one of your own countrymen and love him as yourself—for you were once strangers in Egypt. I am Yahweh your God [Lev. 19:33–34].

Here we see grace dissipating privilege and ownership: the universal breaks into the personal and private to enlarge it with a global dimension.

The coming of a child into a community or conjugal cell is not so that the child may be a prolongation of its parents and, even less, their property. Unbounded respect, in proportion to the love accorded this new and surprising being, is due this stranger.

No process of standardization or domestication should violate the child's otherness, its marvelous and amazing originality. The child holds the promise of a breakthrough into a qualitatively different world, not that the child can, in any way, dispense with grace, but because of the surprise packets of heredity, both the auspicious and the inauspicious. The pedagogy integrated in revolutionary praxis places its wager on a future that will be an improvement on the present, one in which a citizen of the world, newborn and still unknown, can become an artisan cooperating in the never ending effort to achieve full human liberation for all.

And the Christian community, instead of being an odd collection of contiguous atoms is then an infinitely diversified body of couples, celibates, widows, children, the elderly[17]—a living organism continually created and renewed by the Spirit so that it may participate as one in this painful and splendid birthing by revealing to every human being without distinction that the final word in the history of the world, as well as in the venture of Jesus of Nazareth, is the victory of Life.

Chapter 7

The Wind Is Rising

*"The wind is rising: we must prepare
ourselves to survive the storm."*
—Paul Valéry

The theological practice sketched so far is neither easy nor does it carry any guarantee against errors or deviations. That its fundamental focus is correct does not prevent it from either making choices by trial and error or taking long detours to reach an objective. Leaving Egypt behind, the Hebrews did not move in a straight line to the promised land; they went back and forth across the desert for forty years. After a good start comes articulation, the putting together of a historically judicious action, the day-to-day planning to move forward—a series of decisions necessarily relative and ambiguous. In our world the technological progress being made by western Europe is increasingly controlled by the Federal Republic of Germany and is, therefore, firmly tied to American imperialism and constrained by the investments of multinational companies. At the same time, a conversion-breakthrough and the praxis flowing from it are taking place within a counterrevolutionary political, cultural, and ecclesiastical environment. An examination of the general lines that are going to characterize the apparently reformist type of tactic and the revolutionary strategy of militant Christians still has to be made.

From the ecclesial area only three examples of these developments will be presented: practical ecclesiology, eucharistic celebration, and ecumenical action, it being evident that *praxis is determined within political groups, Christians and non-Christians together.*

Militancy and Community

One of the seemingly logical but basically skewed consequences of tracing these lines is going to be an impetus to institute "a church of the left," a partisan community-club. A number of "basic groups" have not steered clear of this reef, envisioning ideological unanimity as a useful commodity for cementing the Christian community together.

To adopt it would mean falling back into all the old errors of institutional authoritarianism and clericalism, whatever the new veneer used to cover them, and so it could not be seriously defended. We must repeat, the praxis-analysis-ideology dialectic—a constitutive element of militant groups, activist bodies, labor unions, political cells and parties—cannot be exclusively or specifically "Christian." This can be seen in joint militant action, in personal contacts, in engagement in unity of a common undertaking: action could never mean uniformity. The rereading of the scriptures, the orientation and critique of praxis in reference to the praxis and critique of Jesus of Nazareth—if these developments can come about in dialogue (in the sense in which dialogue was defined earlier)—take place when Christians involved in different types of militancy gather in order to face up to their actions. Militancy does not exclude plurality, in spite of the difficulties and ambiguities it entails.

These ecclesial regroupings, with their conscious assumption of an ecclesiastical character, are not, for all that, the church. They do not add up to the ecclesial reality of the church, and they are often denied the right to say they belong to it. If they find themselves marginal, they do so in relation to a reality that is, at least empirically, larger than their movements or "small communities," surpassing them in extent, duration, and means of expression.

The sectarian temptation is, as its etymology suggests (from *secare*, "to cut, amputate"), to cut oneself off organically from an ecclesiastical institution. Such a rupture does not create hermits and asocial human beings; for it to have significance, it must come about *in* society, defying its powers from within and openly rejecting the values that it puts forward as its justification. If a rupture takes place, it is up to the great institution to take the initiative; it has experienced no lack of amputations; its historical journey has been strewn with them, leaving it bloodless and cadaverous. Militants take an internal rupture seriously, making a correct reading of a number of gospel passages, particularly the Johannine teachings about a presence *in* the world that is not *of* the world—in other words, a presence that turns away from the practices and values of the dominant society, as the bishops of Brazil have emphasized:

> There are those who put the word of God "My Kingdom is not of this world" (John 18:36) to wrong use. We say that, though the most beautiful part of the kingdom will be lived in the house of our Father, the church knows that the kingdom of God begins here. We must all work to bring it about that persons move from situations that are less human to situations that are more human.[1]

This is the breakthrough that is not a breakaway; it displaces the center of gravity of margination or, to express it more aptly, when marginality is spoken of, it asks the question, Marginal in relation to what? Unquestionably, militants are marginal when faced with matters that institutions have frequently made a specialty of: the *validity* of ecclesiastical actions and the criteria for true ministry; the whole complex of problems that exercise the *apostolate*—the church looking outward, recognizing its relationship to the whole of humanity as the reason for its existence. Then there is the concentration on *apostolicity*, a preoccupation with "Which is the true church? Which is the one that is to be the beacon and magnet bringing the others together?" An enormous literature, produced with a tremendous expenditure of energy, has delivered itself of a mountain of trivial opuscules that have not led to any concrete progress.

Another area, *sexuality*, an important subject in itself, is often used as an alibi for avoiding political issues considered better left untouched. Fortunately, for a long time the Christian masses have just let their bishops, whether celibates or not, expatiate at length on masturbation, homosexuality, and premarital relations as the gravest of sins.

Then there is *ecumenism*, a subject we shall come back to. In many cases, it is nothing more than a marriage between two senior citizens. It can be touching, it may make them happy, but it is foreordained to be without issue. Ecumenism can also find itself embodied in an organization—not a guileless one—that is a consortium for the defense of "spiritual" interests threatened by a rising tide of atheism.

Those militants who did not leave the churches when they were repelled by ecclesiastical ignorance of and aloofness from the actual problems of real persons resolved to accept being mentally and emotionally alienated from the great oral and written debates agitating church assemblies. Militants are to be found elsewhere and at times have the bitter experience of recognizing that their prolonged or progressive estrangement does not much concern institutional centers. These have apparently reversed the parable of the lost sheep, showing little care for the ninety-nine lost in strange places or skirmishing outside the borders of parochial wastelands and, instead of seeking these straying numbers, the churches jealously gather their few conformist chicks under their wings. This grating irony is hardly an exaggeration: any number of witnesses could be brought forward to testify to the depressing facts that substantiate it.

But now, the word "marginal" changes sides; "marginal" is anything unrelated to the lives of the people, anything aside from or neutral toward concrete class struggles. Institutions prefer interclass discourse to the practice of Jesus. Institutions of any and every kind take themselves so seriously and have such an instinct for conservatism and self-preservation that they easily come to consider themselves as the center of reality and define "marginal" in relation to that self-center. But there should be no other central reference point for the churches than the heart and humanity of Jesus.

What ecclesiastics find most difficult to accept is that the frontline of class struggles crosses church borders. Because an entire church is often located "in the North" (see the maps on pp. 100 and 101), on the side of the rich, on the side of institutional violence (even if it is situated in the South!), it then asks, without really wanting to assume the consequences of an answer, what type of relationship is consonant with its mission.

Militants who set their faces against forming partisan groups and, consequently, against cutting themselves off from the institutional body, can do nothing except deliberately take part in a conflictual praxis as the only way of continuing in a communion that is not barren and unreal. The gospel, as a matter of fact, does not eliminate the oppositions that exist between classes; it radicalizes them. To attempt to eradicate conflict would be a futile try at robbing ecclesial existence of all historical reality. We have to assume that oppositions exist in the churches and, if they do not, then we should introduce them there. Militants could not put on a reassuring mask on the pretext that decency demands that they do so at a eucharistic celebration; they come to the occasion as they are and meet their class enemies there, recognizing and naming them as such:

> It is important for Christians never to deny the differences that arise among them, in order to be able to witness to what unites them. Only those who recognize and admit the *opposita* can confess the Lord Jesus.[2]

The more that "small communities" take on a distinctive character and praxis and the longer they refuse to break away from the parent institution—in spite of the burden and bitterness of making a breakthrough—the better their movements can be described in the paragraphs that follow. These, it should be added, are directly in line with the debates being carried on in France among the various trends of a potential movement of Christians for Socialism. It will be remarked that the first requirement concerns militants: from first to last they must be critical of themselves.

1. Everything is to be decided through effective praxis in line with a clear option for one class, praxis in which collectively defined criteria and decisive actions are taken in common.

2. For Christian militants, the church is also a milieu where specific action should be undertaken. This does not mean reduc-

ing the church to a sociological factor or eliminating its other dimensions—relational, spiritual, sacramental, and theological—but rather recognizing that each of these is inseparable from the political role played by the institution as a whole. We need to know that we can never free ourselves from the tension that exists between "mystery" and historical action, between "vocation" and the standardization that marks all institutions. Consequently we should be in complete disagreement with the bishop who said to his council, "There are no problems; there are only mysteries."

Christian militants are, therefore, inevitably caught up in the conflict so aptly described by the German student of theology quoted by J. A. T. Robinson:

> We must try to be at one and the same time *for* the Church and *against* the Church. They alone can serve her faithfully whose consciences are continually exercised as to whether they ought not, for Christ's sake, to leave her.[3]

What is at stake is not just to open up an ideological, countertheological front within institutions and to denounce their compromises but, even more than that, to combat statements and practices that are incompatible with the gospel, and to open breaches through which the practice of Jesus and the dynamic ecclesiality of those who follow him can surge through.

3. The movement, the trend, the approach that I am attempting to describe can have outcomes that could never be programed. One such result was the statement of the conference of Brazilian bishops quoted in the preceding chapter, a clear and courageous position made public. Others occur when some traditional and conformist parish enters into open tension with the established order by taking, for example, the part of foreign workers or political refugees against the civil authorities who serve the dominant classes. This happened at Montpellier in January 1975, when the "forces of order" pushed their way into a Protestant church to drive out more than a hundred Arab migrant workers welcomed there by the Protestant community. The Arabs were conducting a hunger strike to protest measures taken to disperse and expel some of their comrades. The authorities of the Reformed

Church, meeting in Paris at the time, gave their official support to the action taken by the local community under the direction of its leaders.[4]

Ecclesiastical institutions can and sometimes do officially declare their opposition to the death penalty, the sale of arms to foreign countries, the policy of having nuclear plants all over the country. We have seen spectacular financial decisions made by the World Council of Churches to support Third World liberation movements and to oppose racism and militarism. Such deeds honor the hidden and thankless action undertaken by militants within weighty and unwieldy institutions. It could easily be shown that being this kind of presence is more costly and crippling for churches in "socialist countries" or "national security" states; however, what is under discussion here is the situation in western Europe. Within it, in spite of the varied nuances marking it and the risks involved in militant action within institutions, a number of possible avenues for change are still being offered in good times and bad, and it would be stupid to disregard them. And it is important, politically and spiritually, that an institution traditionally allied with the existing economic and political powers should occasionally break away and take a stand in opposition. Such an action may have no tomorrow, but it is significant enough today to be prepared to do it, initiating it, and sending its reverberations through the world as far as they will go.

Militants, for their part, will take care to avoid left-wing institutionalization, as well as despair or resignation when they meet with inertia or opposition. As they undertake the "long march through the institution," they must be on guard against illusion and skepticism, keeping an equal distance from ecclesiastical triumphalism and despondence, moving step by step against a closed and rigid milieu whenever some possibility of penetrating its defenses appears.

4. Institutional praxis affects and moves us for several other reasons. I remember gratefully that an institution put me in contact with Christ, a standardized version of him, to be sure, but a representation that did lead me, through a rereading of the scriptures grounded on praxis, to discover and to engage in my present revolutionary action. I am aware, too, that a number of Christians trapped in institutional alienations can be conscientized and

involved in the militant process and that the "institutional conti-nuity" assured by the longevity of "the larger churches" creates—at the same time as it threatens—adversaries, "informal groups" of militants. The essential thing, however, is that mili-tancy is going to effect, right within institutional churches, a reformulation of the faith, a renewal of celebration, a reappro-priation of the gospel by and for the poor. . . on condition, of course, that minority and marginality do not become some sort of elitism.

5. It is realistic to limit ourselves to these modest hopes and never to expect an ecclesiastical institution as such, whatever its label, to take a clear position in the vanguard of class struggles. Or, to put it in another way, all institutions, in taking any posi-tion, are most often guided not by the interests of the people but by their own preservation and welfare. The primary concern of every institution is to maintain and reproduce itself. This holds true even in so-called socialist countries, where traditional institu-tions, as in Cuba and Vietnam, grudgingly submit to regimes that are the outcomes of revolution and, for the most part, continue to look back longingly to their former privileges; or, as in the U.S.S.R., for example, where they fall in line with the policies of the government in power and, at least as far as their hierarchical leaders are concerned, side with its decisions and see to it that relations with the state are governed by a kind of Constantinian edict analogous to the one made centuries ago.

Be that as it may, revolutionary Christians never expect to be-come bishops or presidents; history is full of examples showing that they are destined to remain in the minority, comprising about 10 percent in the Confessing Church of Germany (under the in-spiring leadership of Karl Barth and Martin Niemöller) and un-doubtedly less than that in North Vietnam before 1954 and in South Vietnam before 1975 and even afterward.

When we come to realize the ponderous political inertia of reli-gious masses that have been walled off and conditioned by leaders whose fundamental anticommunism has always carried greater weight than their opportunism, we can understand, if not justify, the pressures and different administrative measures used by those who now govern, especially if we are careful not to forget that, in the past, these officials were treated, individually and collec-tively, with immeasurably greater harshness than they themselves have exercised since coming into power and that the regimes responsible were openly supported by the churches. Briefly, contrary to the dreams of some and the desires of others, Christian militants are never going to seize ecclesiastical power. At the very most, here and there, one or two of them will have a piece of it as sops to allay the uneasy consciences of bishops, as sureties and excuses for routine but worrisome compromises.

I wonder if militant groups, which are more or less suspect, discriminated against, and decried, are ready to believe that it is the minorities following Jesus in the church and outside it who are the makers of history—provided that they effectively represent the aspirations of the masses and know how to make their voices heard by the powers that be, including the ecclesiastical. The vision of "a people's church" remains a magnanimous and moving utopia, and its effective realization presupposes the establishment of a socialist society that has not as yet been realized anywhere on earth.

Ecclesiality and Conflicts

The practice of making a breakthrough without breaking away leads inevitably to the subject of pluralism and its limits. The General Commission on Evangelization of the Reformed Church of France spoke of it in its report to the national synod of 1976:

> We need to take a good look at what this term, which some delight in and others disparage, comprehends. It admits of gradations: differences, divergencies, oppositions, antagonisms. How far are these capable of remaining together and when do they become irreconcilable? Unquestionably, they can be sustained only if a common identity is preserved and accompanied by a willingness not to dodge problems but to stay with them to the end in *forthright, fraternal confrontation*. Pluralism must be lived in accordance with the gospel and not as tolerance granted to "another gospel" (Gal. 1:9). In what follows pluralism cannot be taken to mean a state of neutrality. Only with a hope that transcends opposition and looks to unity in diversity can pluralism be entered into.

In our present situation, there is always conflict regarding ecclesial practice and tension in comradely unity among those who are sometimes opposed to one another in the name of what is most essential: their respective understandings of the gospel. Pluralism can be lived only under two conditions, and we willingly recognize that doing so is an art both difficult and dangerous:

—a real and perduring recognition of the right to have differences;

—an effort to listen and to hear—that is, to take into account the option of the other as criticizing and limiting our own option.

Radical incompatability—which should not be too quickly assumed—means an irreducible antagonism, a conviction that the other represents and witnesses to an antigospel. Barth provides us with an instance of this when he told German Christians, ''You have another God, another Christ.'' We have an additional example in Christians who refuse to have communion with those who justify torture, racism, or the perpetuation of systems of domination.

The effort to accept the other—which excludes using caricatures and making superficial judgments of the other as well as categorical judgments and authoritarian measures of discipline—cannot take precedence over a reading of the gospel that is not limited to discourse but includes praxis. Those found to be an enemy, on the social or international level, are not less an enemy because they claim to be Christian. At a time when conflicts are becoming radicalized, we ought to come to understand that it is within the churches, too, and perhaps principally within the churches, that we must put into practice the words ''Love your enemies.'' This does not imply either softness or surrender but, rather, on the contrary, an opposition just as resolute as it is inspired by the promise of reconciliation. The church—what an extraordinary gospel presence it could be in the contemporary world!—would then be a place—one of the only places—where adversaries could coexist facing one another openly and at times even coming together around the same table. For that to be achieved, we must not minimize or disguise or deny but recognize the gravity of the conflicts that make us opponents precisely because of our different understandings of the gospel. This will be all the more important if both sides are not to take their stands on positions defined once and for all but to move forward, with the same fidelity, to their common reference point. And the promise given us to remain firm in confrontations is that the Christ proclaimed by apostolic testimony is not "yes and no": he is the liberating *"Yes"* who will in the end triumph over all particularist intransigence by leading us, together with all humankind, to the great Amen of eschatological praise.[5]

The church in our times could acquire a new identity and, in this way, a new and surprising credibility if it took seriously such a position with regard to conflicts, maintaining a loving solidarity with those we confront as enemies. In this way it would be a sign that class struggles, the importance of which today cannot be underestimated, are not an end in themselves. They will come to an end in a universal movement of reconciliation and freedom for all.

RECONCILIATION AND LIBERATION

We are nearing the conclusion of our ecclesiological reflection. We are able to see in sharper definition the contours of the difficult and thankless practice of critical participation in institutional life and of a reflective utilization of the chances and possibilities offered by the most traditional churches. A tactic of working through breaches in institutional walls, of making use of institutional channels to say and do things at variance with the stance of church leaders and prominent Christians on social issues, produces among militants a radical change in Christian lifestyle and in the language used to express what the gospel has to say.

In particular, if love is, first of all, a choice of class, if it consists in opting for solidarity with the downtrodden; if, because of that very fact, love radicalizes conflicts and accepts confrontations within the community itself, it is because love looks at life with realistic clarity, refusing to cover historical specters with a religious fog, never abandoning hope for anybody, even during the worst battles, and leaving killers as well as victims to God's reckoning.

Centuries of idealist ways of thinking and classist compromises have made love seem weak and of little worth. Now love is becoming a sound and salutary presence once more, calling out to the most alienated, attacking the roots of every religious and political betrayal of human beings, moving with unremitting determination to dismantle barriers and tear away masks, to restore a real life to every human being, making it possible for all to discover what it means to be a man or a woman. Once again, we find ourselves surprisingly close to "Che" Guevara:

> Let me say, at the risk of appearing ridiculous, that the true revolutionary is guided by strong feelings of love. It is impossible to think of an authentic revolutionary without this quality. This is perhaps one of the great challenges to leaders; they must combine an impassioned spirit with a cold mind and make painful decisions without flinching. Our vanguard revolutionaries must idealize their love for the people, for the most hallowed causes, and make it one and indivisible. . . .
>
> Revolutionary leaders must have a large dose of humanity, a large dose of a sense of justice and truth to avoid falling into dogmatic extremes, into cold scholasticism, into isolation from the masses. They must struggle every day so that their love of humanity is transformed into concrete deeds, into acts that will serve as an example, a mobilizing factor. . . .[6]

We must always be mindful of the fact that a Marxist is not a kind of torpedo—a fanatical machine set in motion toward a predetermined end by a self-starting mechanism. Fidel addressed himself to this specific problem in one of his speeches:

> Who says that Marxism means renouncing human sentiments, associations, love, respect, concern for comrades? Who says that Marxism means having no soul, no emotions? Indeed it is precisely love for humanity that engendered Marxism, which means love for humanity, for humankind, the desire to work to overcome the wretchedness and injustice suffered by the proletariat, to put an end to their crucifixion, to free them of the whole burden of exploitation weighing them down. Love has brought about the real possibility, and more than that, the historical neces-

sity for the social revolution interpreted by Karl Marx. But what made him that interpreter if not the wealth of human sentiment represented by persons like him and Engels and Lenin?"[7]

Make no mistake, in contrast to the floods of holy eloquence, to all the treatises of mystical theology on love, and to all the idealist discourses on *eros* and *agape* as well, these few sentences present a Marxist and revolutionary praxis of what is contained in the gospel—not sentiment but a "being with and for others." We may refer here again to Dietrich Bonhoeffer and his presentation of Christ as "a man for others," even though a certain ambiguity is latent in this expression because the prisoner of Tegel, an aristocrat and a solitary, had no experience of militant group action and had not undertaken any serious analysis of society. Nor did he have any other vision of the future than the restoration some day of "a better Germany"—that is, of a "correct" capitalist and bourgeois republic.

These obvious limitations in his witness and heroism are precisely what led his readers to go beyond his fragmentary intuitions and to affirm, in regard to this particular point, that persons cannot be *for* others unless they are, first of all, *with* others, in complete solidarity with them, identified with them and committed to them; otherwise, all "being *for*" is tainted with condescension and, perhaps, paternalism as well. In the most classic christologies, the incarnation is what makes liberating action efficacious and real: Christ enters history and, when dying, he is abandoned by others, the ones he came to because he wanted to be their neighbor. Unless we become neighbors, we cannot really "be for" others! What Che and Fidel have to say about partisan love expresses this well.

If love does not risk partisan choices and involvements, it is not universal; or, rather, it is lost in a welter of universal idealism limited to dealing with what is without meaning or force. Because liberating fellowship envisions, beyond itself, a reconciled humankind, because it takes into consideration the real circumstances of human lives—including their divisions—it has meaning and value for the whole world. Without such vision and realism, love is only a coating that serves to hide antagonisms and contradictions, a religious cloud that obscures great conflicts and historical confrontations. Let is be said again, we love persons only by first accepting them in the concrete—that is, as they exist geographically and historically. We love persons only by taking sides with victims against aggressors—quite precisely, by choosing and assuming effective solidarity with a class.

Like the gospel, theology is universal only by being situated, rooted, and involved in time and space. The creative originality of messianic practice in any particular situation reveals its universal scope and all-inclusive schema. We do not postulate the particular by beginning with the universal; we reach the universal by way of infinitely diverse and specific situations, which are not reducible to one another but are all touched and quickened by the salutary action of the subversive of Nazareth. The universal and unique character of the gospel is not an *a priori* dogma but the summation of infinitely varied experiences, never codified, always open to change and, in their diversity, ever converging.

Integrists of all confessions are foolhardy to try to have doctrine and celebration made universally uniform, and they are benighted in considering every adaptation, every translation, every new concretization as perversions. Paradoxically, the very fact that each of us sees ourself in the astonishing identity that the living Jesus communicates to everyone whom he encounters, the very fact that Jesus enters into every situation without converting it into a single stereotype and that he does not diminish others to the status of a mere functionary or permit himself to be so diminished, gives his action and his person their astonishing quality of being otherly and alike, of being for all time and yet contemporary, of belonging under every sky and in all climates, of appearing at home in every age and in every milieu.

The gospel is universal because it challenges and liberates everyone who receives and follows it without excising them from their history, without constraining them or making them wear a mask; it brings together and activates persons of all classes and nations in their particular social, linguistic, cultural, and racial circumstances, taking them seriously just as they are and making it possible for them to become fully themselves in the measure to which they, for their part, accept their share of responsibility for the destiny of the human race.

What is universal is the liberation of all persons so that they realize themselves and speak for themselves. Getting the masses to move forward means summoning everyone to "arise and walk." We become ourselves in the universal uprising of the poor. A twofold movement takes place when an evangelical militant turns away from any narrow self-interest and joins some front of collective struggle with no possibility or desire to turn back. These undertakings are of an infinite variety, depending upon the particular circumstances of the class conflicts they express. No normative typology can be applied to them; the collectivity does not destroy individuals but calls them forth, matures, and enriches them.

This redefinition of the universal through the particular leads to some basic questions about a certain number of accepted religious ideas, and, among others, the thinking about *reconciliation*. This is not the place to make a detailed analysis of that New Testament concept, which is both original and central to it. A few observations will serve. Probably created by St. Paul, it expressed the radical change that happened with the irruption of Jesus of Nazareth into history. Since then nothing has been or can ever be the same. A decisive event took place, an act of liberating solidarity that makes relationships between human beings and God and between human beings themselves *something other* than what they used to be. Everything was empowered with new life—humanity and its world—and the good news was to be received and irradiated.

Later and in our own time, the dominant ideo-theology developed a logic about reconciliation that makes the very heart of it consist in fogging out conflicts and freezing over confrontations—as political powers do when they keep talking about "national reconciliation" when what is at stake is getting rebellious underlings to submit to their masters again, whether that means workers back into their factories or peasants back to their plows or students back into the university—all back to their former tasks once more, and nothing further to be said. As for the clerical line of reasoning about reconciliation, it aims at maintaining things as they are; it rejects class struggles, the denunciation of the historical role of institutions, and political confrontations within the Christian community as contrary to the gospel.

By some marvelous conjuring trick, the most astonishing announcement of the New Testament, the word that proclaims a decisive upheaval, a breakup of old securities and guarantees, and the establishment of entirely new relationships, has been made to serve as a tactical base—with a whole arsenal of reproaches aimed at creating a bad conscience in opponents—for the conservative strategy of the politico-ecclesiastical order. A long time ago most churches opted for the status quo rather than for justice, and they have largely succeeded in persuading Christians that some injustice is, in any case, preferable to disorder. The love of order raised to the rank of a prime value—and all the psycho-political reflexes that the love of order creates—has largely taken precedence over the love of the other and all the risks it implies. This is why there is hardly any term as reviled by militants and by those who have turned their backs on the churches and, sometimes with one and the same stroke, have broken with the gospel, as the word "reconciliation." The sarcasm that greets anybody who ventures to be its advocate indicates the measure of a hostility bordering on hatred. Here is what a young member of the black power movement has to say:

> Be advised, the term we hate above all others in your white oppressor vocabulary is "reconciliation." First of all, it lets it be understood that an original idyllic situation could be reestablished. Now that situation never existed: from the beginning the black has always been the victim, the drudge, and the slave of the white. With nothing changed in our relationships with one another, the word "reconciliation" is thrown at our heads. The black lies prone on the ground with a white knee on his chest while the white talks to the black of love and peace between the races. So I say—*first* take your knee off my chest, let me begin to breathe again and get to my feet, and then we will see if *we* are ready to be reconciled with you. But stop talking about a subject that, as long as justice has not been established by our liberation, is nothing but hateful to us.[8]

AN AFRICAN CHALLENGE

Echoes of the counterviolence of American Black Muslims can be heard in more than one position taken by Canon Burgess Carr, secretary general of the All Africa Conference of Churches.

Preaching at Versailles, December 12, 1976, on Isaiah 40:1–8, he had the following to say:

> *In the Christian tradition,* as the church has falsely interpreted and taught judgment and mercy, they were presented in a way meant to be consoling, as though God's mercy prevails over his judgment. Bonhoeffer was right in describing this tendency in preaching and pastoral ministry as making grace "cheap." Marx rightly called it the "opium of the people."
>
> The text I have chosen is a key to the understanding of these two terms:
>
> —For the oppressed and exploited there is no more consoling message than the announcement that all flesh is grass and that all domination over men and women will disappear.
>
> —What "consoles" them is the downfall of the possessors, the powerful, the well-filled: *"He has pulled down princes* from their thrones *and exalted the lowly. The hungry he has filled with good things,* the rich sent empty away" (Luke 1:52–53). For the poor and the oppressed, "consolation" consists in the proclamation of revolution: the redistribution of power, the reversal of the existing political and economic situation, with those starving for justice filled at last.
>
> There is no "consolation" for those who, according to the criteria of this world, are already filled.
>
> And you, where are you to be found in all this? Are we going to say that God's will is manifested when the youth of Soweto revolt? When liberation movements intensify their struggle for justice and human dignity by driving out their racist oppressors?
>
> I tell you, *judgment* and *mercy* are not two elements counterbalancing each other in a system in which, at the last judgment, equilibrium is established by the added weight of the grace of God, of Jesus Christ and his blood, of the cross, or of saints interceding for us. Mercy, salvation, and liberation are part of the judgment of God. The judgment of God brings mercy to those who are in need of it. God's judgment

is justice for those who have been deprived of justice, and hunger and thirst for it. And the judgment of God is manifested in actions: When God restores rights that have been taken away, justice is established by judgment.

In African theological reflection on liberation, it is important to revive the biblical concept of judgment as the establishment of justice, which, of necessity, means mercy for the oppressed and the loss of power, prestige, and privileges for those who have taken possession of them.[9]

In February 1976, before this talk was given, the Confession of Alexandria spoke of pardon, which, like mercy, is at the heart of the message of reconciliation:

. . . we have turned our eyes away from the structures of injustice in our societies, concentrating our efforts on the survival of our churches as institutions. All too often we have been stumbling blocks for others. We grieve for these sins and many others and ask God to forgive us.

A full understanding of that forgiveness leaves us no other choice than to continue the struggle for the full liberation of all men and women and of their societies as well.

We recognize that political liberation in Africa and in the Near East is part of this liberation. However, the forces in control and the abuse of human rights in the independent countries of Africa make us mindful that we must have a more inclusive, global understanding of the word "liberation." Liberation is, therefore, *an ongoing struggle.* . . .[10]

In an interview in December 1976, Burgess Carr gave a statement of his position that could not have been clearer or more explicit. The scandalized stupefaction of the German Protestant bourgeois public whom he was addressing is understandable:

Question: The All Africa Conference of Churches has stated that revolution is inevitable in southern Africa because the real representatives of the African people have been excluded from the attempt to find a peaceful solution. In another connection, during your stay in France, you have stated that Christians could perhaps come to take up arms in South Africa. The Conference is taking on a very grave responsibility. As its secretary, can you explain this position?

Answer: If we said that the only solution for South Africa is to give serious consideration to engaging in an armed struggle, it is because the situation has developed in a way that makes any other solution impossible. Negotiations for a peaceful solution in southern Africa have not achieved and, we are more and more convinced, will not achieve any positive results. . . .

We have reached the point where we are convinced that we cannot remain slaves. Black persons are the only ones in the world who are still slaves, and slaves in their own country. This is an intolerable situation. It cannot and shall not continue. We are not speaking only of those who have been murdered or massacred in the name of racism and colonialism on our continent in the past. We must be just as courageous today and offer our lives for the children dying in South Africa. We must put an end to this situation. That is the role of the churches—that is, of the African people. The churches are not superstructures. They are not apart from the people. Their members are not Martians. The African churches are the churches of Africans. Their position is clear and the national councils of the Conference simply reflect that position. Africans feel this deeply.

Question: How is your position Christian? Isn't your analysis purely political? How do you as Christians differ from the black governments of Africa?

Answer: I do not understand why you are making a difference between a Christian and a political position. I don't think in dualistic terms. I am an African, a black man. My position as a Christian is no different from my position as a suffering man.

Question: Do you mean that the churches are always to say what the African governments and peoples say?

Answer: What are you calling churches? What are the churches? We do not understand each other because you bring your Western categories and distinctions into the discussion. The church is the people, the African church is the African people. The church is not the institution, or something up in the air, a group of persons uninvolved in the real world. That is not our way of thinking about the church.

I am trying to say at least one thing clearly: when you ask me as a Christian, as a member of the church, as a church leader, if the time has come for armed conflict, I answer yes, because of the judgment we make of the situation in which we find ourselves: our people dominated and oppressed by white racism. The judgment we make is like the judgment you made when you were faced with Hitler. We are facing an evil. You did, too, but it lasted for only a few years, from 1938 to 1945; for us, we have lived with it for three hundred years. And now the time has come to put an end to it. If we allow it to go on until the end of this century and beyond into the twenty-first, then, with the weaponry the government has in its hands, we will never rid ourselves of it. If we let South Africa become a nuclear power—which Germany and France are helping it to become—if we allow it to reinforce racism with nuclear power, that will be the end not only for South Africa but for all the rest of Africa. And blacks, wherever they are, will be lost. . . .[11]

Here we catch a glimpse of what "a people's church" could be, a community making the people's cause wholly its own, belonging to a people that no gospel reference separates in any way from those who do not belong to it. Be that as it may, liberating praxis dispels the disarming talk about reconciliation and a rereading of the Bible implied by that praxis makes it possible to recover the original meaning of the Pauline message: the declaration that God's grace was dearly bought; that mercy is inseparable from the judgment of the cross; that the ambassadors of reconciliation (2 Cor. 5:20) are not to regard justice as of little account; and that the reestablishment of justice is the indispensable condition for the reality of what these ambassadors proclaim. And historical experience offers proof of the message: once liberation has been achieved, a time follows, as in Algeria and Vietnam, when friendship erases the memory of past horrors. It seems that the generosity of the oppressed of yesterday is immeasurably greater than the arbitrary injustice and cruelty of their former masters.

Militancy and Communion

Of all the elements of Christianity, the eucharist has been the most ill-used; not only was its relational character destroyed by replacing a meal with a rite, but the sweeping invitation of Jesus, his welcome to the hungry, and his initiative in sharing bread and acting as host to them all has been turned into a sacred mystery for initiates only. As a consequence, the question of validity and its guarantees have taken on prime importance. Until now, communities, even those of a non-Catholic kind, have not progressed beyond polemical protestations such as "But our eucharist, too, is valid; it is in conformity with what the Lord intended and instituted!" We know well the interminable, vapid, and futile discussions on this subject and all the distinctions made between intercommunion, concelebration, eucharistic hospitality—all so many high-altitude impasses in which theologians and bishops are stuck, grieved and saddened that those on the ground level are often happily indifferent to problems above them.

In their venture to domesticate the eucharist—that permanent breach in the religious ghetto, opening it up to the materially and spiritually hungry[12]—the hierarchies and their theologians have practically reduced the presence of Christ in the eucharist to its localization in the "sacramental species," the bread and wine. In addition, they have, for the most part, preferred an explanation of the modalities of the real presence to an affirmation of the presence itself. Interest in the "how" has relegated the "what" to second place.

As a result, we have mountains of theological treatises on the possibility and the mode of the real presence, and we have endless classic disputes between those who hold for transubstantiation or consubstantiation or spiritual presence or a memorial. And let us not forget the silence of those who, disheartened by these interminable and profitless encounters—and by all the institutional justifications that they cover and disclose—decide not to have any eucharistic doctrine or celebration in their communities. The

Salvation Army, with its paternalistic practice of welcoming and feeding the poor, is very close to the Lord's Supper, although it rejects specific ceremonies. The majority of the churches, on the contrary—leaving aside some exceptional circumstances to which we shall return later—have definitely lost the savor of the Cenacle.

To be sure, some diminution had already begun to take place in the New Testament, particularly in St. John's Gospel, in the passage that a number of exegetes agree came from a Hellenistic catechism (John 6:51–58): The flesh-and-blood language could have been prompted by the need to react against the spiritualist dualism of the surrounding environment. The fact remains that the fourth evangelist formulates his statements on the body-food and blood-drink at the far end of an arc that has its starting point in the account of Jesus' distribution of five loaves of bread and two fish to five thousand hungry persons. (The eucharist had its beginning in a picnic for the people!) Undoubtedly it is also meant to remind us that humanity does not live by bread alone, that its true nourishment is offered in Jesus' gift of himself to the world.

The dominant theology, with the obvious intent of removing everything from the eucharist that presupposes social practice, has retained only the identification of bread-body and wine-blood, but detached from the events and cultures out of which it arose. It is no more than an expression of a primitive magical practice, of necessity a source of the most appalling religious alienations. The sacralization of the matter has taken precedence over the sanctification of those gathered together for worship and celebration. Credentials must be presented and adherence to doctrine formulated by theologians and bishops is demanded—this instead of allowing worshipers to be caught up in a current of liberating and irradiating life.

The fact is, the Pauline and synoptic texts represent another viewpoint: the presence of the Risen One is linked not so much with the elements transformed and utilized as signs or channels of his lasting action in the community but, above all and essentially, in the community gathered together in remembrance and in expectation of him during a meal, which he once took and continues to take anew with his disciples. The bread and wine signify *nothing* apart from the sharing and the historical and eschatological *vision* of the bringing together of the whole hungry human race.

A coming together of those united in Jesus' memory and in anticipation of his liberating return into the world is indeed a celebration by those who are his body—that is, the new humanity, of which he is the head—and his blood—that is, the communicable life that he imparts to every human being. What constitutes the eucharist is not a localized real presence but an existential, communitarian quality expressed in the sharing of bread and wine, recalling *and* actualizing the practice, death, and present life of Jesus. None of us can be in communion with him without being responsible for feeding the multitudes by sharing in their distress and putting what we possess at their disposition. Poverty, struggle, and hope borne in common and lived in remembering and invoking the living Jesus together with the repast that concretizes this communion are the core and meaning of the original eucharist and of the eucharist that is really contemporary today. Apart from that, there can be any number of denuded or overblown liturgies harking back to traditional models or moving on to daring innovations, but all come to nothing. They are tombs, whether simple or ornate, for a dead Jesus.

The eucharistic reality, therefore, transcends the rite. *Every* meal taken while sharing historical responsibilities and fellowship has, for those with eyes to see, eucharistic value; it is a celebration of struggle and hope, in which Christians and non-Christians together *do* the truth and can be regarded as disciples united in messianic practice. Are a specific liturgy and an ordained minister necessary when a militant solicitude for the present and future of humankind is at the heart of the meal? Is not every person working for the downtrodden today the hand of the living Jesus right now? When we receive bread from that hand, have our cup filled by it, are we not reliving Emmaus? Obviously, a serious question does arise—but in an inverse direction—regarding the validity of the eucharistic celebrations of all those religious families that define it by criteria internal to their own groups and largely foreign to anybody except a cleric nurtured in an enclosed environment and trained in scholastic distinctions. As the hungry invade the church, it recovers its center; as the streets move inside, the church regains its credibility and confidence.

One day when Tulio Vinay, the Sicilian evangelist, was taking a meal with workers in the Riesi dockyard, he noticed that he had unconsciously repeated the gestures and pronounced the words of the eucharist. Making Jesus present? Surely not! But retracing the footsteps Jesus first traced in our history. And anyone who has seen the moving Bolivian film *¡Fuera de Aquí!* ("get out of here"), on the infiltration of multinationals into Indian pueblos through the mediation of Protestant sects, cannot, without feeling their whole being shaken, view the scene where the poor, driven out of their homes by cynical mining prospectors, arrive at a village that still remains untouched. Famished and denuded of everything, they are received by the villagers with no questions asked and no problems raised, and they share in what little their hosts have. The joy illuminating the faces of those who give and those who receive is eucharistic joy in its fullness.[13]

We need to go beyond that: entire nations—Cuba and Vietnam, for example—are based on shared poverty, on equality in the division of disposable resources, which rules out both luxury and destitution. Religious skeptics and suspicious members of the bourgeoisie are, sad to say, incapable of perceiving the diffuse but decisive reality of sharing in common, on the strength of the messianic invitation, everything needed for the whole group and each one in the group.

The eucharistic celebration has meaning and vitality only through participation in the practice of Jesus and a public affirmation that we intend to do it and are doing it as his followers. In 1968, on the feast of Pentecost, a group of French Christians and non-Christians who were fully participating together in the great political fiesta of the era, met to celebrate the eucharist. They found themselves at odds with the institutional authorities who, severely or with tears in their voices, reproached them for their disregard of the rules of official ecumenism, and with making partisan political agreement the basis of "their" eucharist. The response given distinguished between two modes of celebrating the repast devised by Jesus: (1) "the eucharist of hope," a coming together in expectation of the eschatological unity of Christians divided by the heavy burden of their historical practices and readings; and (2) "the eucharist of experience," a celebration by disciples united in their fidelity to the people and in their praxis of liberation—in spite of their origins and their ties with different and sometimes opposing institutions. At the present time, a number of Christians waver between these two celebrations and we should refrain from making a hasty judgment on them.[14]

There are numerous evidences that when history irrupts into the most static institutions, "the eucharist of hope" can suddenly become a place for a striking manifestation of the actual presence of Jesus. This can happen, for instance, when some traditional parish opens itself to and participates in a liturgy that expresses solidarity with the persecuted and tortured. Then clearly the words convey the Word, and the celebrants are the cohosts of *the one* Host, and all the usual rites and gestures attest to the passion and victory of *the one* Liberator. For the immeasurably precious time they are together, the participants there know joy, surprise, and invigoration even if, frequently, in the moments that follow, everything falls back again into a state of emptiness and death where nothing reaches them save the resounding voices of oppressors. There need be no hesitancy in maintaining that in "the eucharist of experience" the exodus story continues in the struggles and liberations of the downtrodden and that, in and through them, the Liberator of the world is really at work. His action is, in the most classic sense of the term, the *matter* of the celebration.

At such a eucharist, those coming together are taking a brief respite before returning to the combat; they are situating their battle within the perspective of the historical and eschatological—that is, of integral—liberation. They prophesy it and mobilize themselves once again to help bring about its realization. They understand in Jesus' inviting the crowds to a meal that he is calling all those without whom there is no gospel life or faith—the poor. The invitation that he extends to them lifts them above and beyond themselves: "Give them something to eat yourselves" (Luke 9:13 and parallels). Every eucharist made to serve as an excuse for evading this commandment in the face of heartrending reality is not only vain but blasphemous. The real presence of Jesus is in the presence of his followers *in the real.*

As the following quotation makes clear, what is under consideration here is not an initial awakening to the eucharist but a continuing rediscovery of it in the liberating praxis of the disciples of Jesus that, time and time again, provides its matter:

The more you think about it, the more you recognize that communion at tables is a radical reversal of the established order, a disturbance of a kind that a social revolution itself could never produce, an image of a new earth where justice dwells. There are human beings for whom this aspect of the Last Supper is a source of ineffable happiness because . . . these generous hearts would like to share everything, to live the life of the disinherited, to transform the world, or to die. They are in the grip of a prophetic joy for the time when the table is set for everybody and they are offered the opportunity to take their places among the infirm, the despised, the defeated, to eat the same bread and drink from the same cup.

Are we going to tell these prophets that they have no right to communicate because they have not fully grasped the divine paradox of justification by faith? No, no, for what animates them is the spirit of the Messiah. They see better and more clearly than those who only contemplate Christ above them: they contemplate Christ beside them in the person of their companions. They completely fulfill one of the conditions laid down by the apostle Paul for communicating worthily: they "discern the body of the Lord."[15]

Militancy and Unity

Traditional ecumenical activity has already been largely challenged by what has been said heretofore. If, for example, "the eucharist of experience" is not concerned with either the person of the celebrant (Who is it to be then, if not the militant community, prompted by the hope of the oppressed?) or the doctrinal rectitude of the participants (And what is that if not the living practice of Jesus?), then *nothing* remains of the disciplinary rules of institutions and of the work of the subservient theologians who framed them. What a tremendous release of energies would take place if here and there such a cutoff were to occur: it would be like a first awakening.

More and more writers are beginning to use the term *oikoumene* in its original meaning, "the inhabited world"—the world in its Hellenistic sense; not in the sense of (merely) Christian unity. The New Testament concern for world unity is the motive force for true ecumenism; the unity of Christians is not an end in itself or even a worthwhile objective to attain if it is not an *instrument*—purely and simply that!—serving to bring together scattered humanity, sinfully torn apart into factions by contending interests. Any motivation that does not look outward is foreign to true ecumenism; to put it another way, ecumenism cannot have any self-regarding motives, such as getting stalled ecclesiastical enterprises moving again or organizing a common front of defense against mounting secularization and atheism, or even pursuing studies together. All that is peripheral to the central task: to restore a livable earth and to provide hope for the future. Whatever is not ordered to that primary end is basically of secondary importance and a sorry absurdity when given first place. The church is universal—and ecumenical—only in aiming at and working for the good of all.

We see, then, that ecumenism, in whatever places and forms we find it, must be submitted to the critique of revolutionary practice; everything marginal to that practice is, by that very fact, suspect and unfit to be supported by militants. Militants ordinarily do accept members of all groups, whatever their origins, who are engaged in action for the liberation of humanity and the transformation of society. They are less preoccupied with "orthodoxy" than "orthopraxy." A better way to express that is to say that "orthopraxy" is the basis and sign of a right understanding of the gospel. Militants can then have a calm indifference to spectacular but secondary undertakings, and can develop deeper and deeper rootedness in effective practices of militant action for the poor, whoever and wherever they may be. They possess as well, within the most diverse institutional cadres, a creative daring in the celebration and reformulation of the faith.

This gift is accompanied by a serene watchfulness over Christian communities of all confessional colors as well as ecumenical bodies at all levels. Let a program to combat racism or a course of action in favor of human rights or a radical critique of militarism and the arms race appear—even if they originate in institutions marked by the ambiguities of those largely pursuing a course seconded by the dominant theology—they are noticed and gain support. Then too a ferment works in ecumenical fellowship, and here and there many a church fully integrated within some oppressive system may prove to be the one place of freedom still open to the poor, a place where they can speak, pray, and act for prisoners and against torture, can receive sustenance, and, above all, can find themselves accepted as whole persons. Any disregard for, as well as any ignorance of, opportunities offered by ecumenical discussions betrays a lack of revolutionary consciousness and, as a consequence, results in bad praxis. When a conflict is going on, any support, any possibility for utilizing the contradictions in a system, or any other allied strategy, is not to be neglected. Revolutionaries of the Third World have understood this better than have Europeans, and that is why they have taken an active part from the start in the life of ecumenical movements and have had a strong influence on the directions they have taken.

Something further needs to be said: In an era when the world is being exploited by imperialist powers and their multinational companies, only revolutionary ecumenism—that is, unified action by all those who have a worldwide aim and a praxis grounded in liberative militancy—can confront and resist exploiters and deal them blow for blow, clearing the way to a democratic future. This outcome has already been realized to a great extent in a number of socialist countries and of national labor unions, and it should not lack the support of any militant Christian. Algeria, Vietnam, Angola, theaters of spectacular liberations, are, in this eighth decade of the twentieth century, ecumenical loci just as decisive and, doubtless, much more so than such places as Uppsala, the Vatican, and Nairobi, which stake out landmarks along the interminable route to Christian unity. Czechoslovakia, Iran, the United States, and others with or after them should also be among those loci. Little by little a new definition of ecumenism is being worked out: it is the practical multinational solidarity of persons of all ideologies and faiths united for the liberation of their brothers and sisters who are still enslaved anywhere in the world.[16]

Lived in this way by militants throughout the world, ecumenism would give a striking foresight and a real promise of the goal it cannot reach, and that the New Testament calls the kingdom of God.

A Clear Hope

To conclude this chapter and to flesh out the chart on page 176—a sort of inventory showing how the various constituent elements of ecclesiastical institutions and political realities correspond to one another—the following points ought to be emphasized:

1. The synthesis outlined makes no claim to be exhaustive or definitive. It will have fulfilled its purpose if it moves readers to reflect, to take an accurate reading of the course they are following, and to bring it into line with the ends they are seeking. Such as it is, the schema seems to make some sense of many experiences within institutional life as well as the relationship of institutional life to politics. No malice has had any place in its genesis; it was undertaken with the desire to summarize as accurately as possible the findings of inquiries pursued over several decades. And the exceptions to the general profile that show up here and there, if they call for some flexibility in the classifications, do not, for all that, cancel out their consistency and permanence.

2. Are any further protestations needed? The analyses presented do not contain any message of withdrawal, of estrangement from the ecclesial reality. They have been thought out and formulated as so many expressions of a vibrant love for the church. If, as it has been said all too often, the church has, over the centuries, prostituted itself in every imaginable and even unimaginable way, if the spouse and handmaid has too many times metamorphosed into a cruel stepmother or an inhumane nurse to the little ones of the family, nevertheless my solidarity with it remains unbroken. And nothing will break it. Numerous as those are who have left, my wager is to stay with it, not only for the

reasons of political expediency that I have treated at length, but also because I cannot denounce its perfidies as if I were not, in more than one way, responsible for them, or as if, having over and over again known forgiveness myself, I could finally and fully despair of the church.

What I am saying is not some sort of musty idealism but an essential dimension of the praxis of militant Christians: the conviction that God does not abandon any of us, whether as individuals or as groups. And, if grace means anything, it is surely justification—that is, the conversion and newness of life granted to those who once turned their backs on the gospel. And yet, can institutions repent of the compromises that they have made? Can they cut themselves off from their culpable liaisons? And can those enthralled and corrupted by power renounce it? Experience hardly inclines us to indulge in optimistic fancies.[17]

Against this background, words are not enough to satisfy us. What Dietrich Bonhoeffer said about grace keeps coming to mind: grace is not *easy*; it is not to be had like the young man or woman who give themselves to anybody; grace is not *cheap*, it cannot be bought at a low price. There is good reason then for purposely radical analyses and relentless questioning. These ought to have some proportion to the sufferings of dominated men and women, dominated peoples, and to the hope bound up with what could be a communitarian practice of the gospel. Here you find the explanation of my persistent advocacy of making a break that is not a breakaway. Perhaps the passionate plea that opens the book of the prophet Hosea has an echo here. And the one who echoes the plaint is the first one to whom it applies. If such be the case, then these lines will have done their part in the rejection of all religious alibis, all failures to respond to the call of worldwide liberation and to persevere in the steadfast and not necessarily vain expectation that the Christian community will occasionally put off the uniforms of the powerful and the livery of torturers in order to stand among the multitudes as a militant servant, a disinterested liberator, a presence of the risen Jesus. When that happens, a miracle takes place—the kind of miracle that Niemöller salutes with the words, "The church has died; the church is risen!"

CONSTITUENT ELEMENTS OF ECCLESIASTICAL INSTITUTIONS

Outstanding feature	Authoritarian	Pietistic/Charismatic	Pragmatic	Self-managing
structures and borders	hierarchy, discipline (obedience, repetition) / uniformity	organizational flexibility, spiritual firmness / conformity to a model Christian typology	organizational firmness, spiritual anarchy / pluralism	fraternal ecclesiality (liberty, creativity, equality) plurality
practice and spirituality	fanaticism (theologico-political orthodoxy)	fervor and legalistic interiority (evasion of history)	"fluctuating orthodoxy," pantheon of the divinities of conformism	love-struggle (liberative sharing and solidarity)
theology/countertheology	an unchanging god as the guarantor of order	a god of individual fulfillment	intellectualism, tolerance (skepticism)	God of communion and creator of history
their role	justification	intimidation for the sake of the faith	reproductions of the system	evangelical interpretation of praxis
scripture	tradition and magisterium	fundamentalism and illuminism	from historico-critical reading to faith as the key of interpretation	a materialist reading
eucharist	ritualism (validity) reserved for true believers	an emotional zenith reserved for the converted	a religious act without involvement—"eucharistic hospitality"	a prophetic and mobilizing repast open to all
ecumenism	"the great return"	*ecclesiolae in ecclesia*, invisible church, eschatological unity	dialogues, communal activities and services	"secular ecumenism"
politics	fascism	the established order, preferably nonrevolutionary	capitalism, reformism	socialism

DOMINANT THEOLOGIES

No attempt is made here to indicate relationships of cause and effect or interdependence, but simply to indicate correspondences.

May those reading my words realize the love of the poor that fills them, the same love that gives life to the praxis that they recount. I accept being measured and judged by that praxis. May readers realize that my love is also addressed to the church, incalculably poor as it is with its unjust riches and inordinate pretensions. The church is ever being urged to return to its own raison d'être, the origin of its birth and of its new rebirth: the love that puts an end to everything that robs persons of life and humanity, the love that is stronger than death; the life-giving force of the one who rose from the dead.

Epilogue:

A Provisional Evaluation

Any theology is inductive insofar as it reflects some sort of social practice. The ideas that it conveys do not, contrary to its claims, "fall from the skies," but come from a partial and partisan reading of biblical and traditional texts with an eye to promoting the interests to which the theology gives practical service. Tell me what your theology is, and I will tell you what your class option is, and vice versa. As a general rule, that reasoning is valid, taking into consideration that both on the right and on the left inconsistencies and irrelevancies are to be found, and to ignore them is to condemn yourself to unproductive oversimplification and even to contradictions. I have attempted to clarify the relationship between praxis and Christian discourse and to bring about a maximum of coherence between them. It has been a difficult undertaking because no model is to be had, and examples are in short supply. Unquestionably, however, research is moving more and more in this direction, whether it aims to justify the conservative line of the dominant theology or, as in the present case, essays a political critique of the traditional ideo-theology and a critical reading of the practice of Christian militants.

Instead of sacralization—at best a sort of vacuum cleaning of the structures and values of the established order—let us have sanctification, the transformation of existence by the living presence of the Risen One within the struggles carried on for the people. Instead of immobility, let us have the continuous creativity of revolutionary praxis adopting and realizing messianic practice.

Patently, we have not progressed beyond some preliminary steps, and continuing this enterprise would require fuller development and, therefore, further reflection. At this juncture let it suffice to make three points clear. If there is a need to dissipate misunderstandings, these points should contribute to that end:

1. There is no question of idealizing revolutionary praxis and success. For a century and a half, the path of socialism has been deeply marked with enough errors, failures, deformations, and atrocities to keep socialists sober and humble. From beginning to end, revolutionary action is an enormous risk, and there is no guarantee that it will succeed. On the other hand, maintaining the status quo offers little save death and burial. The way leading to the liberation of the oppressed and the birth of a new humanity is dangerous and decisive. Wagering on life and the future is always madness, but this insanity appears immeasurably more evangelical than resignation and passivity, than that accommodation with the intolerable that characterizes "the wisdom of nations" and religious persons in its service. Even if socialism, in its historical realizations, had accumulated as many enormities and monstrosities as Christianity has committed during two thousand years, there would be no reason to condemn the one or the other. The wager is that there will be, as far as each of them is concerned, a sufficiently youthful dynamic to keep disrupting cumbersome institutions, to clear away roadblocks, and to get movement toward the future started again.

A militant Christian could not, through discouragement or disenchantment, relapse into capitalism—which sometimes likes to offer gilded prisons to those whom it has defeated but does not consider altogether irredeemable (This time you are still useful, but don't do it again!) nor ready to be incarcerated in national or Olympic stadiums. A militant Christian could not give up in despair and take refuge in personal agnosticism or in a traditional form of popular religion. The only response to be made to setbacks and defeats is to reject negativism absolutely and to analyze the errors made in order to work out the best policy possible, deepening the conviction that hope will prevail. According to a famous motto, success does not determine perseverance.

2. The theological counterdiscourse sketched in this work has its origin and impetus in the practice of class struggles. The ques-

tion is to know whether or not revolutionary praxis and its corresponding ideology call into question the human and meaningful experience of encountering Jesus of Nazareth and expressing the faith that comes of that encounter. A whole chorus of bishops, pastors, and those who have fellowship in religion rather than in Christ warns those who hold to the option at the source of every materialist reading, "Do this too often, and you will have no specific identity left." Well, no, not really. Non-Christian militants are not going to become confused about who they are and neither are those who, although they used to be traditional Christians, have taken the road to liberating solidarities and are making all the breakthroughs it entails.

What in the dominant ideo-theology often becomes a deadening burden—to the extent that a number of traditional Christians can no longer put up with the society (cultural or not!) of persons like themselves—dies and rises again in joyous, passionate, and completely believable, if paradoxical, new life through revolutionary praxis. Any apologetical attempt to use Christianity as a means of attacking the weak spots of Marxism is abandoned. Dietrich Bonhoeffer denounced that abuse as absurd, base, and unchristian. An apologetic of that kind operates in ignorance of the true dimension of the convictions that are part of the militancy of non-Christians, and knows nothing of the strength that they communicate to militants even under torture and in the face of death. The letters of Gabriel Péri and Jacques Decour ought to be read and reread by Christians, including any who believe themselves in the vanguard of militant action and thought.

In the *Contribution to the Critique of Hegel's Philosophy of Right,* when speaking of the critique of "religious distress," Marx writes of the imaginary flowers that disguise human bondage:

> Criticism has plucked the imaginary flowers from the chains not so that man will wear the chains but so that he will shake off the chains and cull the living flowers.[1]

What does that mean if not that "religious distress" ought no longer to serve as a mask for "real distress"? When human beings have become conscious of a situation of exploitation, oppression, and alienation and have, through fighting for liberation, managed to throw off their chains, what living flowers will they be able to cull? Flowers of human happiness or of meaning offered by a religion revived by revolutionary praxis? There is no need to make a choice between the two: the meaning grasped through encountering Jesus is inseparable from the great and contagious happiness that draws its tremendous significance and scope from that encounter.

3. The glow of this twofold and unique passion animates this book: in every authentic praxis the practice of Jesus, the radiant person of Jesus, appears, always closer, infinitely subversive and liberating, unique and yet reflected on millions of faces, each one a fascinating element in an immense human mosaic.

Ibn Arabi showed astonishing intuition in saying, "Those struck with the malady called Jesus are incurable." Nor have they any desire to be cured, for the wound or body blow dealt to their egoism and will to power will thereafter prevent them from running away to avoid other persons, to elude God, or to escape from themselves. It will oblige them to stay with others, in the midst of the crowd, with and for all of them. It will make it possible for them to receive and to give, to be loved and to love, to be free in order to free others and by freeing others to remain free. Che Guevara, in his own way, says this very well:

Christians should opt definitively for the revolution. . . . But in the revolutionary struggle Christians cannot presume to impose their own dogmas or to proselytize for their churches. They must come without any intention of evangelizing Marxists and without cowardly concealing their faith to assimilate themselves to the latter.

When Christians dare to give full-fledged revolutionary witness, then the . . . revolution will be invincible; because up to now Christians have allowed their doctrine to be used as a tool by reactionaries.[2]

Pascal was not far afield when he wrote in his *Memorial,* "Christ is in agony until the end of the world . . . that is engaged forever in the final struggle! This is no time for us to be sleeping."

Appendix

Documents for Theological Research

Diverse documents have marked the successive stages of research that have led to the publication of this book. Some of them have been included only implicitly, or have received insufficient acknowledgment. That is why I am adding here a selection that may prove a useful contribution to future theological research.

I

In 1972 the synods of the French Reformed and Lutheran (non-concordatarian) Churches decided to undertake a vast reform of theological studies. Merging the two theological faculties of Paris and Montpellier, they founded the Protestant Institute of Theology. The following text is an attempt to describe briefly to young students the underlying intention of the new orientation given to theological training.

Articulation of Reflection on Experience

In the Report on the Reform of Theological Studies we read:

It seems that theology cannot be reduced to an abstract theoretical analysis of revealed truth (even if it be scientifically acceptable), but that in formulating it attention must be paid to life experience.

This text defines the two approaches to theological research, those taken respectively by deductive and inductive theology, which are in competition, and frequently in conflict, throughout the world.

The deductive approach sets out from scripture or from the confessions of faith to extract a body of practical implications for the present time, the service of the gospel and its transmission. It finds its justification in orthodoxy. The inductive approach attempts a spiritual reading of lived experience. It assembles and coordinates experimental data and tries to decipher the biblical message in their light, so as to discover its deep meaning and to avoid its pitfalls. It finds its justification in orthopraxis.

Both share the desire to create a close union between doctrine and action. But whereas deductive theology insists that a sound theological basis and an enlightened faith are necessary as the principle of correct action, inductive theology insists on a responsible involvement in human history, similar to that of Christ himself, as the prerequisite for a vital theology and faith rooted in reality. The former will try to discover the practical consequences, what happens when faith conducts a reflection on faith and when the word is announced and lived in a given situation; inductive theology will apply itself to studying the outside influences that have a decisive effect on the way Christians reason and the way they act.

In both cases we are confronted with a theology seen in relationship to a given situation; in the first case the problem is to translate the gospel into a language that will gain a hearing; in the second case the gospel is to be understood and applied in the light of concrete human commitments, which are, in their turn, interpreted by a new reading of scripture.

There is no doubt that the second way of going about it was really, historically, the first. Nothing can be less systematized than the Bible. Composed from one end to the other of circumstantial narratives, it bears witness to the fact that Israel first of all, and then the church, had the clear intention to interpret its history in the light of its conviction—or let us say its faith—that it was led by God. The Israelites began by leaving Egypt, and then they said: "It was Yahweh who delivered us!" Christians began by meeting Jesus of Nazareth, and then they proclaimed that he was the Christ. After the formation of the canon of the scriptures,

Christians set out to read it, and to explain and systematize it. The interpretation of the written word took the place of the reading of history. Thus the approach of cleric and literary scholars took the place of that of the prophets and builders of history, and it is sometimes thought that this latter approach can be dispensed with.

Theology as taught in seminaries and university faculties is traditionally deductive. Its reputation is based upon its claim to be a science that it taught and studied in a climate where fidelity to the past in no way excludes a concern for contemporary needs. At the heart of this tension, and traversing it, we find respect for historical events and the doctrine of the incarnation.

Our reform is above all an attempt to give the inductive approach is place in the training that forms the future ministers of the church, and to incorporate in it their lifelong need of reform.

What is at stake is a process of confrontation and reinterpretation of everyday human lives and the witness of scripture. Throughout the process we must take care not to confound the word of God with a given situation, or a given situation with the word, but we try never to take one into account without the other.

Concretely: we shall come to know a situation, analyze it on every level, penetrate it from within and assume it into our lives. We shall then become aware of and sort out a certain number of questions. We shall discover some blind alleys and some challenges, some cases of injustice and some reasons for hope. We shall begin to master problems of language, communication, and behavior in the complexity of their different dimensions. The indispensable discipline will consist in going forward without hesitation in an untiring effort to listen and to understand with as open a mind as possible. The "method of sympathy" ("suffer with") is doubtless the only one that will really open up the road to knowledge.

Then will arise a certain number of demands: simple cries for help or clearly formulated questions. The inductive approach will assume them without diminishing or distorting their meaning, and try to confront them with the gospel, with the love and justice of God, with Christ's ministry and liberation, with pardon, reconciliation, and salvation as the Spirit warrants.

We are not looking for ready-made answers or easy solutions. On the contrary, we must be ready to be knocked about and disturbed in order to undergo the experience of "consoled despair" and or "mobilizing certitude," in which Luther situated the risk and the joy of a faith freed of all the securities and illusions of prefabricated religion, in order to be put to the service of humankind.

There are no magic formulas, only the will to search the gospel from the point of view of a given situation or of concrete responsibilities, and to allow it to challenge you in return. The aim is that, having at the outset better understood the meaning of the gospel, you will be able to live it better in the context of the work you are doing or about to do, or with regard to a socio-professional experience that you have carefully analyzed.

March 15, 1974

II

In 1974, a consultation called by the Commission of the Churches for Peace and Development (CCPD) of the World Council of Churches studied the enormous problem of "domination and dependency." The participants, who came from throughout the world, were invited specifically to reflect upon the historical roles and recent evolutions of the ideologies within their respective continents. The following text is part of the report presented by the consultation.

New Tendencies of West European Theology

TOWARD A THEOLOGY WITHIN PRAXIS

Everything started with the spiritual resistance against Nazism and the struggle of the Confessing German Church. The theology of Karl Barth, himself a committed Social Democrat, had a political impact which is still valid: the analogical relationship between justification and justice; the radical relativity of all powers by the affirmation of the unique lordship of God; the rediscovery of the prophetic role of the Christian community vis-à-vis and within the civil community. More and more political theologies and consciously political theologians appeared. Encounters of confrontation and dialogue with representatives of various political parties and ideological tendencies took place. Militant practical engagement, participation in public life in contradiction and solidarity, resistance against various governmental, military, colonialist, and imperialist enterprises resulted in two complementary conclusions: (1) the discovery of the characteristics of the production of theological discourse; (2) the socio-political role of most of the theologies.

Sifting through all the ideological critique, it appears, in effect, that all dominant theology is an integral part of the ideological production carried on by the dominant classes. Its role in serving to maintain the established order is in direct relationship with its aristocratic conception of the individual, its devaluation of historical relativity, its assistance to authoritarian church structures—or at least their hierarchical, pyramidal organization—their defensive attitudes and distrustful reflexes concerning all popular movements. Preaching and teaching are addressed to the affluent who are exhorted to generosity toward the poor, near or far (various diaconal works, fainthearted campaigns in favor of "aid to the Third World"). However, existent structures are practically never put into question, nor is there any call for a new society constructed by the oppressed. Generally, one can say that theology is the ideological product of the middle classes whose most daring representatives hope that the existing order will improve, but not be radically changed. This theology is entirely of the academic type: it is a product of a classist culture, largely conformist, strongly marked by the doctrinal and sociological clericalism of those who elaborate it in institutions that are extremely authoritarian and opposed to change.

Participation in popular struggles for the independence of oppressed peoples necessarily led those for whom this was a decisive political engagement to denounce the classist character of most European theologies. Whether they remained Christian, or, more likely, rediscovered a Christian reference within their revolutionary engagement, they searched for theological formulations coherent with their praxis of anticapitalist and anti-imperialist struggle. Enlightened by black theology and the liberation theology of Latin America, they have undertaken a reflection on the faith within their own particular socio-ecclesiastical context. This is an effort that is still in its early stages. Their minority character is obvious and their legitimacy is forever put into question by official Christianity.

The following elements can be discerned:

1) If the gospel emerges at the motivational level that leads to taking up a clear position inside national and international class struggles, it is the praxis of solidarity with the oppressed that is decisive. This makes clear that the ideological frontier, that of class struggles, passes through the churches and that no "Christian unity" can serve to hide this reality. Moreover, the ecclesiological practice of revolutionary Christians can be only that of contradiction and confrontation in communion.

2) This praxis is a decisive fact that becomes a true epistemological and hermeneutical principle: as it is reread in effective solidarity with the dominated and in participation with their struggles, the gospel is gradually stripped of the Constantinian gaudery in which it was dressed. It reappears as the good news of liberation-salvation, of the end of oppression, and of the realistic possibility and hope for a world of justice. An "areligious" reading of the gospel becomes normal—that is, as Bonhoeffer presented and lived it: a political reading. Everything is brought into focus by placing traditional Christian affirmations in the context of concrete, local engagements within the general growth of humanity.

3) Thus, theology is a "second act" in regard to this praxis. Theology is evangelical reflection that sizes up praxis in its true dimensions, revealing at the same time its limits and its eschatological aims. Because all ideologies tend to absolutize themselves and the will for power is always a risk for militancy, theology will be able to play the role of a critic and put "the person for others" and "being with others" at the heart of a militancy inseparable from the oppressed masses and always attentive to them.

4) Criticism of the institutional churches, of their compromises with oppressive powers, and of their role in ideological blockade, is the indispensable counterpart of a rediscovery of the gospel reread with the eyes of the poor. In the Third World perspective, the need for a radical questioning of missionary values and methods is evident.

Theologies that have a certain number of characteristics in common are now surfacing everywhere in Europe:

1) They are inductive and incomplete, in necessary contrast with the grand global edifices of the deductive theologies.

2) They are popular—of the people—not only because they

correspond with the aspirations and with the sufferings of the poor but also because they are no longer the privilege of clerics and specialists. They are elaborated in the struggle and research of men and women,[2] of pastors and priests, of specialists and amateurs.

3) They are ecumenical, not only because they ignore confessional barriers, but above all because they have a planetary vision of liberative confrontations and because they consider the unity of Christians only as an instrument to serve the unity of humanity as a whole. Christian unity is sometimes a consequence of "secular" unity.

4) They are based on dialogue, for they receive and retransmit the appeals of numerous non-Christians and make use of analytical instruments and of "secular" mediations.

5) They assume with tranquility their character of countertheology, manifesting the present sundered character of the Christian community, tearing down false facades and aiming at a unity beyond the conflicts of the present, in a world where oppressed and oppressors will be able to be reconciled because systems of oppression will be destroyed and just societies will make it possible for all to live in freedom.

October 3, 1974

III

In the autumn of 1974, the Universal Federation of Christian Student Associations held a European conference in Lillehammer, Norway. At the end of this meeting, which was overshadowed by the last public executions ordered by the Franco regime in its death throes, the following text, proposed as an account of the work accomplished, was voted to be included among the documents of the conference.

The Witness of the Gospel
in the Class Struggle for Socialism

1) The crisis and the crimes of international capitalism are its condemnation. Incapable of bringing a solution to the problems that are decisive for the future of humankind, it nevertheless sur-

vives, obliging the majority of those whose lives it controls to accept a growing state of underdevelopment: the aim of giving everyone access to a minimum of household and consumer goods has long since been abandoned. Nobody hesitates to qualify whole countries, regions, and populations as "below the poverty line"—and destined to remain that way. The developed countries need the cheap material resources and the cheap labor they can get from the poor. They exploit them pitilessly, with the complicity of totalitarian regimes for whom torture and terror are routine methods of government.

2) We have decided—some of us a long time ago, others only recently—to become actively involved in the fight against a system that has given abundant proof of its incompetence and its cynicism. We are aware that natural resources are running out, pollution has gone beyond danger levels, and the demographic explosion has not ended. In view of these facts we believe that without a radical transformation of the structures of production, power, and the sharing of wealth, the human race is condemned to disappear, and we have chosen the socialist approach as the only way out.

3) We affirm this choice in full awareness of the deformation and the contradictions of a certain number of socialist regimes. We are certain that, whatever successes capitalism may have achieved, it leads to a cruel deadlock, whereas socialism, despite the errors and the crimes that are committed in its name, opens a new path toward a future marked by more freedom and more justice.

4) In practice we are committed to the struggle that the oppressed classes are waging against those who dominate them, because we are convinced that peace and reconciliation are impossible as long as a privileged minority can deprive the masses of their rights and the wages they are entitled to, and exploit them limitlessly. Class struggle is not a diversionary tactic, but the very framework of our action and our reflection; we cannot absent ourselves from it and we have no desire to do so. We are involved side by side with those who are fighting for a better world.

5) In this struggle the great ecclesiastical institutions (and their "scientific" theologians) are to be found in the ranks of our adversaries. They are most frequently docile instruments of the financial powers, political systems, and ideological weapons of

the ruling classes. In most of our countries, religion sacralizes the established order of which it has become a part. In consequence we oppose it, convinced that clericalism has been, and still is, one of the principal factors in the enslavement of human beings.

6) Despite the opinion that one might glean from the Christian communities to which we belong and desire to remain attached, daily experience teaches us that the gospel is a force of subversive energy: it bursts open ghettos and destroys inhuman principles; it is a stimulant to adopt new, creative lifestyles that promote the cause of freedom. Jesus of Nazareth is still alive among us; he leads us off with him to construct a society in which everything will be shared and all will take an active part in leading the world forward, where freedom will no longer be a luxury reserved to a select few, but the daily bread of all.

7) To believe in Jesus does not entail giving up taking a full part in class struggles. On the contrary, it leads us to radicalize our struggle, hoping for the day when it will be over and meanwhile working to hasten its coming.

IV

An ecumenical study group from three continents (Africa, Latin America, and Southern Europe) was planned to meet at Figueira da Foz, Portugal, toward the end of the summer of 1976. During the preceding spring all the participants were invited to send in a contribution on the theme, "a new humankind."

The New Humankind

Whenever this topic comes up for discussion today, tremors of irritation and hope are always to be felt in the air. Some sneer incredulously: "Nonsense! The human being will always be the same, an impenitent sinner past praying for." But others feel that this is the real issue at stake throughout history, and that no changes will ever be decisive as long as humankind has not been changed in the very roots of its being.

It is remarkable that both primitive Christianity and primitive Marxism proclaimed a utopian message and spoke of a renewed humankind. For Christians it was to be ushered in by the kingdom of God and individual conversion, for Marxists by the revolution.

In both instances societies of a substantially different type were to follow. In time, both sides got down to organizing the conquests made by the first generation. The framework and structures of government were set up, battles were fought within and without the institution, and disciplinary and dogmatic rules became more stringent.

Then came the test of power. Both Christianity and Marxism seem to have envisaged power with the same lighthearted optimism, ignoring the heavy weight it brings with it and the perversions it can lead to—whether self-initiated or other-initiated. Deformations of clericalism and bureaucracy are expressions of the congenital weakness of Christianity and Marxism faced with the test of power. This weakness has two forms: the inability to control power and the inability to assure its renewal. In both camps, the disappearance of hope and of a real desire to see a new humankind emerge is at the same time the cause and the consequence of their repeated defeats by power, whether used by others against them or within their reach to grasp.

The irritation mentioned above is the expression of a deep feeling of unsuccess. Hope, on the contrary, expresses the conviction that there are, in Christianity as in Marxism, enough resources to overcome the errors and deviations that have marked their realizations throughout history.

Paradoxically, enthusiasm for the utopia of a renewed humankind has always arisen on the outskirts of these two great currents of thought. The centers of religious and ideological authority have always accused these utopian minorities of heresy or deviationism, denying, in effect, that the birth of the new humankind is the objective of history and the ultimate meaning of witness and militancy. But they have never been able to prevent groups of persons, more or less numerous and representative, from trying again and again to assist in the birth of a new humankind.

At the present time the mainline churches are being challenged on this point by charismatic or critical groups that have grown up on their borders and retain close bonds with them. In the Marxist family, revolutions that have taken place in the Third World, far from "the fatherland of the revolution" and in declared tension with it, have made the new humanity a central point in their collective efforts at all levels. This is the substantial difference between the socialist countries of Europe and the regimes of Vietnam, China, Cuba, and Mozambique. Has the Old World given up hoping that there can be anything new under the sun?

The tragedy of Europe is its penchant for dualism, dichotomy. Christianity has insistently refused to undertake a critical and creative reflection in the social and political fields, because of the clerical agreements by which it is bound to the powers that be, each side having accepted substantial losses in exchange for some apparent advantages. That is why it has most often given preference to individualistic interiority, making personal achievement and personal salvation the heart of its specific message and the justification of its existence. Marxism, on the other hand, was born atheistic, by reason of its unavoidable confrontation with the historical forms of a Christianity bound to the most repressive feudal or capitalistic structures. And it has historically fought shy of "humanism," considered to be the ideology of the regimes it was out to destroy. As a result it has appeared as a form of economic theory, often purely mechanical. In taking over political power, it sets no goals for itself beyond the transformation of social structures and modes of production.

If European Christianity often appears to be concerned first and foremost with favoring the emergence of a person "with clean hands, but really no hands at all" (Péguy), Marxism on our continent has lost sight of the "cultural" dimension of human life. It has often "built a socialist house"—and this is no trifling achievement, indeed it has often been remarkable—"but there is no socialist person to live in it" (J. Hromadka). To unpolitical ethics (in reality perfectly integrated with and subject to the order of those in power), Marxism has opposed politics without ethics, demanding unconditional submission to the organs of power, and even going so far as to consider those who oppose the regime psychologically abnormal and candidates for special psychiatric treatment. Will the Third World deliver us of this lamentable mutual sterilization?

The materialist reading of the Bible and the interpretation of Marxism in the light of the gospel mean, on the one hand, ongoing clarification of the backgrounds and the economic and political consequences of each historical achievement of Christianity and, on the other hand, an insistence on the equal importance of each of the three "powers"—economic, political, and ideological—and on their autonomy with respect to one another. For both camps it means refusing all claims to infallibility, all dogmatism, and all predigested decisions. This much being acquired, we can also formulate the following remarks:

1) The reason why Marxism is continually put in dialectical tension with the gospel message is because it is considered the best instrument we have to make an adequate analysis of our societies, and to furnish means capable of transforming them radically. At the very outset of the new awareness that it initiates is the recognition of the reality of class struggle, apart from which it is useless to speak about a "new humankind."

2) The new humanity is at once a collective and personal being, universal and particular. Any attempt to accelerate its appearance at the present time while ignoring one of these two dimensions will result in the mutilations that we have already mentioned. But if we are called to define priorities, we should make the difficult wager that social transformations, by creating equality between oppressors and oppressed, will give all persons the best opportunity to achieve the fullness of their human potential. But this is never a matter of course, an automatic result; it remains a risk, a mystery, perhaps even a miracle.

3) If the new humankind has a universal, fully ecumenical dimension, it cannot appear in full until the whole world has achieved freedom. Today, at best, it can appear only partially. It still has to defend itself against the attacks directed against it, and also to organize attacks against those who, in other parts of the world, obstruct the forward march of other peoples to new birth. That is why violence, destined to disappear completely from the life of the new humankind, is still a historical necessity, animated by national and international solidarities. Such solidarity is the criterion by which we can test the authenticity of the new humankind emerging today, fragmentary though it be.

4) Where the new humankind begins to emerge, it must be on its guard against inhuman deviations. If it does not have a clear awareness of the temptations and pitfalls of power, it may die aborning. The oppressed of today can become the tyrants of tomorrow. The tragedy of Stalin is a warning to all who become

involved in revolutionary activity, be they Christians or Marxists: only those who are themselves freed from the desire for power dare take the risk of destroying and taking over the power wrongly used by others. This is the prophetic judgment on the folly of anarchism. On the one hand, only those who commit themselves to a struggle for freedom are really freed in their inner selves; on the other hand, only the action of those who are freed from all ambition and personal self-seeking can be truly liberating. Many Marxists recognize this today; and Jesus teaches that the greatest among us is to be the servant of all.

5) Like all births, that of the new humankind takes place amid blood and suffering: the death of Christ on the cross, and that of so many heroes who gave their lives so that others might live. As certain great modern witnesses remind us emphatically—Camilo Torres, Ernesto "Che" Guevara, Martin Luther King—there is no place for triumphalism here. Those alone can work for a revolutionary evangelization and for a human revolution who accept that their militancy or their witness be associated with sacrifice and with carrying the cross. Today we can give only some rough indications of what the new human person will be like when it emerges. Only the resurrection will manifest it in its cosmic truth.

6) Nevertheless, while "waiting for this time and hastening its coming," it is possible to give some provisional indications, which are synthesized in the chart on page 196. Fernando Belo has drawn our attention to the "threefold nature of the messianic practice of Jesus"—the use of hands: sharing, the economic dimension of love; the use of feet: breaking down barriers, the political dimension of hope; the use of the eyes, prophetic penetration, the ideological dimension of faith. Where all this exists, the new humankind is present. Where someone provokes a deliberate rupture with a class situation and gets involved in a class position on the side of the oppressed, the new human person is present. Wherever persons refuse to be subjected to others, or to subject others to themselves, and they begin to build together, to manage their affairs and to share together, the new humankind is present. If faith consists in recognizing the new human person in the person of Jesus, it also consists in deciphering his action in history.

7) The new humanity also infers that the wisdom and the folly

3 spaces of activity → 3 levels of analysis ↓	SOCIETY	CULTURE	CHURCH
ECONOMIC	SELF-MANAGING opposed to multinationals; economic development at the service of cultural development EQUALITY	OPEN TO ALL struggle against unequal division of labor; labor equilibrium; equilibrium assured between tasks on the collective and personal level	SHARING BREAD solidarity in short- and long-term relationships; open and dynamic eucharist
POLITICAL	NEW TYPES OF LIBERATION worldwide solidarity; socialist internationalism DEMOCRATIC CONTROL AND RENEWAL OF POWER STRUCTURES	COMMITTED BUT NOT DOGMATIC at the service of a freed society that has not become sectarian or discriminative or manipulative	HISTORY ENTERED INTO AND READ IN THE LIGHT OF THE GOSPEL exercise of prophetic responsibility; free Christians standing on their own feet
IDEOLOGICAL	CULTURAL REVOLUTION permanent criticism of social values; "being" is considered more important than "having"	PROMISES AND DANGERS OF CREATIVITY both collective and personal THE UTOPIAS OF NEW SOCIETIES	HOPE AND CELEBRATION criticism of theologies based on order, of Constantinian clericalism, of the many forms taken by a "reinvestment of religious sentiment"

This chart is meant to be provocative. We realize perfectly well that it could have been designed differently. Consider it relative and imperfect, but—we hope—suggestive. And if you criticize it, may your criticism be useful to all of us.

of Western intellectuals—"our" Christianity and "our" Marxism—are going to be jostled by our colleagues from Africa, from Latin America—and why not also from Olde Europe? After that meeting and confrontation we shall no longer be quite the same: they will have helped us to be born anew.

8) There is a final and very serious point to make. Wherever the new humankind emerges, women will be in full equality with men (as in Vietnam, above all). In European societies, which are scandalously and stupidly masculine, "the other half of heaven" is a decisive test for the reality of the new humanity. In saying this we lament the fact that in our study group women were admitted in homeopathic doses. Is the "ecumenical new humankind" to be hemiplegic?[3]

V

The next two texts can be said to pertain to the order of "spirituality." They are included here to show that revolutionary praxis and a materialist reading of the scriptures do not necessarily diminish or do away with outward expressions of faith, such as celebration and prayer.

The first text is the response I wrote to an immense correspondence I received after the sermon I preached on Easter Sunday morning in 1976. The sermon was broadcast on French radio by the Protestant Federation.

Easter 1976

As Robert MacNamara, former defense secretary of the U.S.A. and then president of the World Bank, said in a speech he gave in Nairobi on September 24, 1974, half of the two billion human beings who live in the underdeveloped countries suffer from hunger or malnutrition. Approximately 20 to 25 percent of the children there die before reaching the age of five. Among those who survive, thousands lead a curtailed life because of brain damage, growth arrest, and reduced vitality due to insufficient nourishment. Eight hundred million of them cannot read or write. Despite advances in education, we must expect that illiteracy will be even more prevalent among their children. The average span of life in the underdeveloped countries is twenty years less than in the rich countries. A third of the world population (that living in the industrialized countries) disposes of seven-eighths of the total income of the world; the other two-thirds have to make do with the remaining eighth.

To believe, to live, and to proclaim Easter cannot mean forgetting these realities. Either our belief in the presence and the action of the risen Lord changes something in *that* situation and changes it *now,* or else our understanding of the Easter narrative is nothing more than that of an old wives' tale meant to comfort some holy souls worried about eternity.

Nowhere does the New Testament narrate what happened at the moment of the resurrection, but *everywhere* it sheds light on manifestations of it in everyday life today. And conversion, which was its surprising effect in my life, is inseparable from the certitude with which we await "the new heavens and the new earth, where righteousness will be at home." But how can we live today, full of this hope, except by working to make *this* world *different?* For there can be no religious escape from, or solitary happiness in communion with, Jesus risen from the dead.

Easter means refusing to allow hymns to the risen Lord to drown out the sobbing of the abandoned and the cries of the tortured, or to draw attention away from the silence of the hungry— which reports in daily newspapers and on television, as well as the publications of, for example, Amnesty International, transmit to those who do not close their minds to them. So I shall sing no alleluias that serve as alibis for not caring about death in all types of regimes everywhere in the world. The more I meditate on the victory of Christ over death, the more I shall struggle against all that is intolerable in the world of today, the more I shall study it and denounce what causes it.

The only good news for me is that which is *first of all* good news for the poor and the oppressed to whom it announces the end of oppression, *and also* for those in power, to whom it gives a solemn warning: they will be brought down from their thrones and privileges, and will at last be able to become comrades and helpmates. Denounced as their accomplice, I can receive pardon, and I must show it by working for the establishment of a new world together with the numerous unbelievers who also live the values of the resurrection without realizing it. Then alone will Easter joy and praises ring true.

If Easter does not mean the rout of all the forces of death, it is a horrible mockery. If conversion is not expressed by taking a firm stand, in both word and deed, against everything that assaults human life, it is nothing more than an alienating drug for those who dream of heaven while doing their best to forget this world or despairing of it. If the resurrection is not the all-directional irruption of seemingly impossible and improbable life, of a resolute will to create a better future for all, then it is just an empty and useless word.

It is clear that a world where there is more justice and more freedom is not yet the kingdom of God; but it is also evident that such a world is the necessary expression of an active hope that the kingdom will come. Eduard Thurneysen used to say: "to fail to do certain things would be to fail the kingdom of God." Easter is to undertake projects because we have hope; it is to persevere in spite of failure and death; it is to refuse to resign oneself to evil and misfortune; it is to put one's stakes on the victories of life, even if they are always provisional and uncertain, believing that life will always have the last word in the history of each one of us, as in the collective adventure of the human race.

My joy is to live and proclaim Easter in this way, with my many companions for whom faith is also the strength and motive force behind political responsibility—that is to say, the daily struggle of those who are on their feet.

I must not hide the fact that for me this is realized in practice by militancy for socialism. This by no means signifies that I am blind with respect to the errors or the crimes of regimes that claim to be socialist: I have long since openly taken a stand against Stalinism, the invasion of Czechoslovakia, and special treatment in psychiatric hospitals. Nevertheless I hold, together with the Protestant Federation among others, that a dictatorial regime that employs torture is even more horrible when its representatives claim that they do so in order to defend Christian civilization.

May 8, 1976

VI

I wrote the following text at the request of the Christian Association for the Abolition of Torture. Its members wanted to know what a—reputedly leftist—theologian would have to say about action programs taken up by Christians against torture.

Torture and Prayer

I am not a "religious" person. Or, if you prefer, I am not naturally pious. That is simply how it is: I am neither sad about it nor proud.

That explains why prayer is, for me, more like Luke's parable of the three friends (chap. 11) than Matthew's description of a dialogue in secret (chap. 6). Life, its circumstances and its struggles, lead me again and again to the point where I cannot do anything but cry "help!" Not just for myself—I try to manage somehow—but for all those with whom I am engaged in the struggle for the future of humankind, including those who are in prison, delivered up to the sadism of brutes or of scientists with warped minds—those I cannot join, or free, or relieve. If I could, I would forever make the rounds, going from one prison to another and from one camp and special hospital to another in those hundred or so countries where torture is the rule in the (mal)treatment of political prisoners—sometimes even of ordinary prisoners.

Intercession is thus the only means at my disposal for escaping the imprisonment of my inability to act, to break through space, barbed wire, and the doors of the cells of those held incommunicado or in isolation. Intercession is not an alibi for any kind of passivity; it is the continuation of the struggle with other means; it is the indispensable prolongation of political action and of participation in class struggle on the side of all victims of exploitation and domination. It is an act of modesty, not of demobilization, the expression of lucid realism, not of discouragement, even less of any sort of resignation. What matters is that I am always conscious of both the indispensable character and the relativity of the work in which I am engaged with others. While waiting for that great final liberation, small steps, limited advances, can be made toward greater justice and respect for human life in *this* world in which we live. As long as I breathe, I will not rest or be indifferent toward the imprisoned—those I know and those I do not know—who are reduced to the last moral and physical extremity. But I know that I shall not live to see the end of the agony of human beings martyred by other human beings. Even if I lived a thousand years, I know that no political progress will make it disappear completely. There will always be victims and executioners.

Medicine and political action have something in common: you fight an enemy that you will never defeat completely. Even the best society imaginable will not be composed of persons with hearts ruled solely by love and a passion for justice.[4] And here is the place for intercession: it is possible to help the tortured by embracing them in universal prayer, asking the Father to establish the kingdom on earth where the will of God be done, as in heaven.

All activists encounter obstacles; all fighters know the precariousness of victory; all politicians know the ambiguity of success and the tragedy of the provisional, the dramatic transience of even the finest achievement, and the terrible perversions of power. To intercede is to renounce neither daily efforts nor historical hope; it is to go beyond both toward the true goal of all life: the new heaven and the new earth where justice prevails.

Thus, the more I act, and act militantly, take sides and struggle, the more intercession becomes the indispensable prolongation, and even the nerve and corrective, of a political involvement that has been knowingly entered into and continually radicalized.

Among those for whom I am called to mediate before God—as the only one who can really respond to their distress—are the tortured, under whatsoever regime. To pray for them means, first of all, that they experience in their midst the presence of the Crucified, their brother, their neighbor, their fellow human being. When I am without injury or fetters, his proximity is not evident to me; but the day I am sick or a prisoner, delivered up to insecurity and arbitrariness, he is there, with and in me. This is the staggering message of the great prophecy in Matthew 25 and, even in the midst of happiness and joy, I want never to lose my remembrance of and concern for the millions of brothers and sisters who, in the North, South, East, and West, act out again in our history the story of his passion. How can I see it, believe it, confess it, if I do not remain in unbroken solidarity with them—through the struggles of politics and prayer?

"Jesus Christ is in agony until the end of the world," says Pascal. And if I was once suspicious of this affirmation and of the glorification of suffering that it encourages, I know today what this truly means—through the evidence collected by the Russell Tribunal and Amnesty International, as well as through many accounts of those who survived Nazi or Russian concentration camps. It is so evident that sometimes even a nonbeliever has an intimation of this mysterious and very real companionship: "Do you think Christ really suffered as much as this?" a young fellow prisoner said to Roland de Pury at Fort Montluc in Lyons in 1942, where there was no torture, at least not consciously intended. But Pascal adds: "One must not sleep during that time." During this period, the discovery of or encounter with Christ never means individual satisfaction, a pause or a period of repose. I do not grasp at him—no! I am seized by him only in the renunciation of any thought of disengagement or retreat. I am thrown, as a consequence, into an active and intelligent *practice* of solidarity. Inasmuch as Jesus Christ refuses to come down from the cross, he asks me to set free all those who are martyred today and who are his brothers and sisters. The uniqueness of his innocent sacrifice implies opposition to its being repeated on others.

The struggle against torture is also the struggle *for* the executioners, against the systems of which they too are victims and prisoner-accomplices. The recent "Communication to the People of God" of the National Conference of Brazilian Bishops offers a strong reminder:

> In the face of facts that arouse public indignation, we cannot attribute the responsibility for this situation entirely to the local policeman who presses the trigger of his revolver, or to any other policeman or soldier. We have to look deeper to find the roots of what makes this climate of violence possible.
>
> In the arena of evil, not everybody is a "wolf in sheep's clothing." There are some with good intention who are there out of ignorance, like Saul who persecuted the Chris-

tians, or like the centurion at the execution of Christ. There are even those who sincerely mean to serve the cause of good and "to serve God." That is why, when they make one of our brothers or sisters suffer, we must not entertain a desire for revenge or wish that God would punish them. We must pray for them as Christ did: "Father, forgive them, for they know not what they do." Our struggle is not directed against persons: they are all worthy of our love. Our struggle is against the bondage of sin, of hunger, and of injustice for which these persons are responsible, even if unconsciously.[5]

Indeed, solidarity with the tortured, in communion with the Crucified, implies prayer for the executioners. It excludes hatred of others, whoever they may be, and reserves it for the systems, structures, and classes that all over the world, anonymously, with monstrous and cold objectivity, are responsible for inhuman, intolerable outrages. Intercession looks beyond this present time to a reconciled and peaceful world, where victims and executioners are at long last liberated, the former from torture suffered, the latter from torture inflicted; the former knowing what they suffer, the latter often ignorant of the suffering they cause. This in no way excludes what is necessary for justice and punishment, but these must not be part of the spiral of revenge and violence that imprisons nations in a bloody impasse. Those who have been tortured hate torture; only those who have not suffered—and, alas, sometimes those who have suffered "too much"—succumb to the desire to cause suffering. In this, as in many other instances, the Vietnamese teach us a striking lesson: they refrain from revenge, knowing that, in order to construct their future, no contribution whatsoever, even that of those who have been torturers, is to be rejected.

The cross of Christ, the cross of the tortured, speaks of love; it gathers together persons to whom forgiveness—which is never forgetful of the past or contemptuous of justice—has given a freedom that as is improbable as it is unexpected. All the great witnesses who have opposed torture, from Ho Chi Minh to Martin Luther King, and including Martin Niemöller, "Che" Guevara, Eduardo Mondlane, Josef Hromadka, Camilo Torres, and Amilcar Cabral—to name just a few contemporaries—have been convinced that it was necessary to break the fatal chain of violence, terrorism, repression, and revenge. It is not simply the victory of victims over their oppressors, but the establishment of new relationships between peoples and individuals that is the content and framework of intercession, as of every authentic revolutionary struggle.

Active solidarity, joint struggle, and intercession find expression in praise, wonder, and amazement at the refusal of individuals and countries to let themselves be enslaved and degraded, reduced to silence and resignation. What the tortured teach us, paradoxically, is to make ours the surprising affirmation of Psalm 139: "I thank you for the wonder of myself" (v. 14). The woman who sang while being tortured told us before the Russell Tribunal: "I resisted to the end, for if they managed to make me give up, they would have been lost. And then, what great desire to live one has when one is on the side of Truth." These, and so many others (whether Christians or not is of little importance), have helped us discover who we are and who we could be; they allow us to touch with our fingertips the concrete reality of God's promises; one cannot live in their company without continually being led to acts of thanksgiving and praise.

I am aware that I have often spoken in the first person singular—out of honesty, in order to give account of my journeying, my suffering, my joy. I would not want to write a single word, especially not here, that I have not lived in my innermost being. May God forgive me if this is not so. But I know that the most personal prayer is always communitarian: "*Our* Father." So all I want to do is to insert myself into the prayer life of the people of God. Through the centuries it confesses its sins, intercedes for others, and sings the praise of God who leads humankind to the happy end of a history full of tears and blood, of faithfulness and courage.

November 20, 1976

By Way of a Bibliography

Please have no expectations of a list of reference works. They are usually found on the final page or so of a book. Authors use it to establish themselves, to show that they are being scientific. I speak from experience, having climbed my way up several university degrees. Sometimes, nonetheless, a bibliography is, rather than an academic convention, an expression of filiation or solidarity. In the present instance, a good number of citations, on previous pages, assume that role.

It would be a contradiction to this whole book for me to end with the conventional bibliography. In any case, what I want to say and have tried to say from start to finish is that the matter for us to interpret, the book we are never done reading but must always take up again and again and go on reading, is history—that is, life with its infinitely varied practices and, among them, unique and yet communicable, the practice of Jesus of Nazareth.

So, if here at the end, major sources are to be named, then in addition to the three or four mentioned in the body of the work, I shall say that the practices of CIMADE (on behalf of migrants and refugees), of the People's Evangelical Mission in France, and of the international movement of Christians for Socialism (a deplorable but de facto title!)—with all their twists and turns and tensions—are the ones that have challenged, accompanied, and enlightened me along a route with clear historical and eschatological goals but with approaches that are sometimes obscure. I should recall the venture of the movement called Exchange and Dialogue with the hope it brought us and the deception it left with us. And if personal names must be given, these would be, first of all, those of two octogenarians. The first is Martin Niemöller, an unconditional witness for human life against all the "cold monsters," fascist states and bureaucracies, including those that are abusively irresponsible (such as the Federal Republic of Germany, where democracy is foundering in a witch hunt and the religion of national security). The second octogenarian I should name is Marie-Dominique Chenu, the youngest at heart and the most clear-sighted of all European theologians.

To continue with a list of sources, others are Luis Xirinacs, sentry at the gates of the Modelo prison in Barcelona; Giovanni Franzoni, who did not consider his position as abbot of St. Paul Outside-the-Walls as a privilege or honor to be defended at all costs; Gilbert Nicolas, off to Mururoa by boat with a wild plan to prevent a nuclear explosion; Guy Luzsensky and the community of Boquen (they too are "outside the walls," marginated like so many others by institutional authoritarianism) constantly arousing hope for a people's church.

We also have the Portuguese militants who did not give up during fifty years of the worst kind of clerical dictatorship; the authors and signatories of the "Charter of the 77," protesting the intolerable oppression suffered by the people of Czechoslovakia; Lelio Basso, the recipient of great responsibilities and high honors, who is dedicating all his time and what health he still has to the struggle for freedom and human rights. Add to these a great number of well-known and unknown combatants, members of German student groups, whether Christian or not, who endure suspicion, calumny, and discrimination because they do not conform to the new Western order; crowds of antinuclear and workers' rights demonstrators; students of theology putting their stake in the liberating power of the gospel; Jean-Jacques de Félice and his colleagues in the legal profession who are always in the forefront of political trials; Vital Michalon, dying before Creys-Malville; and Elizabeth Käsemann, who was assassinated in Buenos Aires. Just as there are more scholars living at present than during the whole previous history of learning, so are there more martyrs for truth and human freedom right now than from the beginning of Christianity until today.

It is good to live at a time when it costs much to be a militant. Dietrich Bonhoeffer has already reminded us that authentic grace cannot be "cheap."

I have purposely mentioned only Europeans. It is *here* that we are going to show whether or not we have come to understand that neutrality is impossible. It is here that new practices, of necessity animated by those of militants the world over and tactically as well as strategically articulated with them, are to become the occasion of countertheological elaborations. Of these, the present text is but a sample.

If I go on naming other names, I shall have to write a whole new book. So I will close by mentioning only the name of Maurício López, to whom I have dedicated this work. He symbolizes the struggle of all those whose aims are the same as mine. The actions of these groups are our essential texts and our sources. "Reading them"—that is, taking part in combat with them, sharing their risks—is the only grid that makes it possible for us to decipher the countless writings of militants of the past and of the present and, among them, the collection of testimonies given by those who have hoped for and have encountered Jesus of Nazareth.

Notes

Introduction

1. *Le Monde,* Feb. 9, 1972, observed that the signatories who de-nounced "L'Eglise et les pouvoirs" as "biased" and "debatable" be-longed to both orthodox and liberal trends or, better, to both "tradi-tionalists" and "modernists," including a variety of Pietists, Freemasons, and representatives of Lutheran and Calvinist leadership circles. Ultimately we are going to see the notion of "heresy" applied to this work and others that take the same tack.

2. The Ecumenical Institute for the Development of Peoples (IN-ODEP), Paris, was founded in 1970 in line with the principles of Paulo Freire, its first president. It is a center for sharing a variety of experiences and of articulating the activities of militant groups on five continents.

Chapter 1: Flowers among the Ruins

1. *Über Walter Benjamin* (Frankfurt am Main: Suhrkamp, 1968), pp. 72–73.

2. Professor of dogmatics at St. Edmund's College, Ware, pertaining to the Archdiocese of Westminster.

3. Oct. 1963, pp. 307–16.

4. See H. Richard Niebuhr, *The Purpose of the Church and its Minis-try* (New York: Harper & Row, 1956), pp. 80–90.

5. J. A. T. Robinson, *The New Reformation* (London: SCM Press, 1965), pp. 60–63.

6. See *Théologie pastorale ou Théologie du ministère évangélique* (Lausanne: Payot, 1942). A little fishing in this work produces some matchless pearls: "If anyone has been an ideal man, by that very fact he has been an ideal pastor; for it is impossible that being a pastor is not part of being an ideal man, impossible that the one in whom the perfection of human nature is represented, has not been a pastor" (p. 17). "He repro-duced all of Jesus Christ, save his merits" (p. 20). Sad to say, these ro-mantic and excessive ideas have served as a basis for the formation of

thousands of French-speaking Protestant theologians and lay persons. Exactly like Catholic statements on the priesthood, they have united with them to nourish a de facto clericalism that has deeply perverted the practical ecclesiology of the churches of the Reformation.

7. "Les missionaires américaines, victimes de la C.I.A.," *Informations catholiques internationales* 477 (April 1, 1975): 10 ff.

8. *Writings of the Young Marx on Philosophy and Society,* ed. and trans., Lloyd D. Easton and Kurt H. Guddat (Garden City, N.Y.: Doubleday, Anchor Books), p. 438.

9. Names of two Amerindian gods.

10. Text from Instituto de Asesoría antropológica por la Región Maya, San Cristóbal, Chiapas, Mexico.

11. Michel Clévenot, "Histoire de l'église ou histoire des chrétiens," *La Lettre* 220:16.

12. *Vatican II: Points de vue de théologiens protestants* (Paris: Cerf, 1967), pp. 239 ff.

13. Marcel Lefebvre is a French bishop who, after Vatican II, became the leader of a conservative splinter group. He now lives in Switzerland.

14. Robinson, *New Reformation,* p. 54.

15. Ibid., p. 54.

16. Ibid., p. 63.

17. *Le Monde,* March 18, 1972, p. 14.

18. *New Reformation,* pp. 61-62.

19. Quoted by Roger Garaudy in *De l'anathème au dialogue* (Paris: Plon, 1965), p. 12.

20. Karl Marx, *Contribution to the Critique of Hegel's Philosophy of Right* (New York: Schocken Books, 1964), p. 57.

21. See Pablo Richard, *Origine et développement du mouvement "Chrétiens pour le socialisme"* (Paris: Centre Lebret, 1976), pp. 38 ff.

Chapter 2: The Writing of History

1. M. Caratini and P. Grandjean, *Le Statut des missions en Indochine* (Paris: Librairie de recueil Sirey, 1943 [?]), p. 82.

2. Text furnished by the Comité national des catholiques, Hanoi.

3. "Human Relations among the Populations of South Africa in the Light of Holy Scripture," in *Reformierte Kirchen im Südafrikanischen Vielvölkerstaat* (Pretoria: Nederduits-gereformeerde Kerk, 1976), p. 75.

4. Italics added to emphasize especially significant passages.

5. "Statement of the Ecumenical Dialogue of Third World Theologians," *World Parish* 17:153, March 1977; also in Sergio Torres and Virginia Fabella, eds., *The Emergent Gospel* (Maryknoll, N.Y.: Orbis, 1978), pp. 265-67.

6. A system of values designed to conceal social reality and to oblige the masses to accept passively the structures that dominate them.

7. *Politique et foi* (Strasbourg: Cerdic, 1972), pp. 121 ff.

8. Ibid.

9. Harvey Cox, *God's Revolution and Man's Responsibility* (Valley Forge, Pa.: Judson, 1965), pp. 39–49.

10. Oscar Cullmann, *Christology of the New Testament* (Philadelphia: Westminster, 1964), chap. 3, pp. 65, 73–81; chap. 7, pp. 207–33.

11. Abbé Pierre is a French Catholic priest who was also a member of Parliament, but resigned his seat in the House of Deputies shortly after World War II in order to found a movement of help for the Fourth World, based on the recuperation of recyclable materials (*Les Chiffonniers d'Emmaüs*). Later he was also an advocate of twinning between French and African towns and was active in organizing help for Bangladesh.

12. An allusion to a passage from Kant in favor of revolution as "essentially moral."

13. From a letter in 1801 to Roederer, Napoleon's confidant and a member of his Council of State, in Adrien Dansette, ed., *Napoléon, pensées politiques et sociales* (Paris: Flammarion, 1969), p. 146.

14. Gerhard von Rad, *Old Testament Theology* (New York: Harper & Row, 1962), pp. 178–79, 296–305.

15. Paul Ricoeur, "La critique de la religion et le langage de la foi," *Bulletin du Centre Protestant d'Etudes* (Geneva, 1964).

16. Roger Garaudy, *Pour vous qui est Jésus-Christ?* (Paris: Cerf, 1971), pp. 111 ff.

17. Official English version, CFS National Office, Detroit, Michigan.

18. "Paths Towards a New Experience of Faith," First International Encounter of CFS, CFS National Office, Detroit.

19. "Théologies noires et latino-américaines de libération," *Parole et Société,* April 1973.

20. *J'avoue que j'ai vécu* (Paris: Gallimard, 1975).

Chapter 3: The Four Dimensions of Hermeneutics

1. Paul Ricoeur, "La critique de la religion et le langage de la foi," *Bulletin du Centre Protestant d'Etudes* (Geneva, 1964).

2. Ibid.

3. See Karl Barth, *Dogmatique*, vol. III, tome 2, ch. II, pp. 130ff. (Geneva: Labor et Fides, 1961).

4. Fernando Belo, *A Materialist Reading of the Gospel of Mark* (Maryknoll, N.Y.: Orbis, 1981), p. 286.

5. Ricoeur, "La critique de la religion."

6. Richard Stauffer, "L'aile gauche de la Réforme ou la Réforme radicale," *Hokma* (March 1976): 1 ff.

7. Paul Ricoeur, "Urbanisation et sécularisation," *Christianisme social* (1967): 333.

Chapter 4: Reading in Tune or out of Tune with the Times

1. Gustavo Gutiérrez, "Origine et histoire de la théologie de la libération" (Centre de recherche théologique missionnaire, 1973), p. 2.

2. Barth made a clear statement concerning his militancy in a final interview recorded by Roswita Schmalenbach, November 10, 1968 (EVZ, LP 30217).

3. Hugo Assmann, "Théologies noires et latino-americaines de libération," *Parole et Societe* (April 1973): 505 f. Italics added.

4. "Statement of the Ecumenical Dialogue of Third World Theologians," *World Parish* 17: 153 (March 1977); Sergio Torres and Virginia Fabella, eds., *The Emergent Gospel* (Maryknoll, N.Y.: Orbis, 1978), pp. 269–70. Italics added.

5. Assmann, "Théologies noires," p. 501.

6. Fernando Belo, *Lecture matérialiste de l'évangile de Marc* (Paris: Cerf, 1974), p. 13; *A Materialist Reading of the Gospel of Mark* (Maryknoll, N.Y.: Orbis, 1981), p. 1.

7. See Fernando Belo, "Lettre du Portugal," *La Lettre* 212 (April 1976): 4 ff.

8. Belo, *A Materialist Reading,* pp. 247, 253.

9. Karl Marx, *Contribution to the Critique of Hegel's Philosophy of Right,* "On Religion" (New York: Schocken, 1964), p. 42.

10. Charles Birch, "Creation, Technology, and Human Survival," Document no. A1, WCC Publications Service.

Chapter 5: Labels and Uniforms

1. See Renaud de la Taille, "Une carte du monde avec les vraies surfaces," *Science et Vie* (July 1977): 54 ff.

2. Frantz Fanon and Albert Memmi have done brilliant work in bringing this out. Their books, *The Wretched of the Earth* (New York: Grove, 1964), and *The Colonizer and the Colonized* (New York: Orion, 1965), respectively, are classics for militant groups.

3. See Gustavo Gutiérrez, *Origine et histoire de la théologie de libération* (Centre de recherche théologique missionnaire, 1973), pp. 7 ff.

4. *The Essentials of Marx* (New York: Vanguard, 1926), p. 31.

5. Helmut Gollwitzer, "L'heure du prolétariat mondial," *Parole et Société* (1975): 285.

6. A quantity of up-to-date and important information exists on the subject. This includes the reports in the indispensable bulletins of DIAL (Paris), esp. no. 298. See too *Notre Combat* 93 (November 1976), with an article on Marcel Lefebvre, "Les vrais enjeux," as well as "Un pion au service d'une stratégie internationale." Also Joseph Comblin, *Le pouvoir militaire en Amérique latine: L'idéologie de la Sécurité Nationale* (Paris: Ed. Universitaires, 1977), and *The Church and the National Security State* (Maryknoll, N.Y.: Orbis Books).

7. "Pastoral Message to the People of God," National Conference of Brazilian Bishops, 15 November 1976. *Catholic Mind* 85, no. 1312 (April 1977): 55–64.

8. *Christianisme social* (1970): 624 ff.

9. Dom Hélder Câmara, "St. Thomas, Aristotle, Karl Marx," *Parole et societe* (1975): 168.

10. José Ramos-Regidor, "La figura di Gesù e i cristiani marxisti," *Ulisse* 13, fasc. 81 (March 1976): 154–55.

11. Giulio Girardi, *Christianisme, libération humaine et lutte des classes* (Paris: Cerf, 1972), p. 179. Hierarchies are hardly apt to forgive a statement of this kind. Turned out everywhere, Girardi was thereafter suspended from the exercise of his priestly duties.

12. See "Morte e utopia," *Utopia,* (June 1973).

13. "Quel Christianisme, quel marxisme?" *La Lettre* 224 (April 1977): 15 ff.

14. "Paths Toward a New Experience of Faith," document of the first workshop at the International Conference of Christians for Socialism, Quebec, April 13, 1975, ch.2, pp. 66ff.

Chapter 6: Families

1. "The Communist Manifesto" in *The Essentials of Marx* (New York: Vanguard, 1926), pp. 48–49.

2. Paul Ricoeur, "Le socius et le prochain," *Christianisme social* (1960): 461–62.

3. Paris: Centurion; Geneva, Labor et Fides, 1975.

4. André Burguière, *Nouvel Observateur* 626: 83.

5. Paris, Lethielleux, 1963.

6. Told to me by the priest in question.

7. *Les murs ont la parole* (Paris: Tchou, 1968).

8. Ibid.

9. Ibid.

10. Ibid.

11. Roger Mehl, "La révolte étudiante," *Foi et Vie* (1968), no. 4: 36. *Boite* ("box") is the French slang expression for a business firm.

12. Jean Bosc, Olivier Clément, Marie-Joseph Le Guillou, "La crise de mai, essai de discernement chrétien," *Foi et Vie* (1968), no. 3: 4–5.

13. Kurt Tucholsky, *Zwischen Gestern und Morgen* (Hamburg: Rowohlt Reinbeck, 1952), p. 93.

14. Albert Camus, *The Plague* (New York: Random House, Modern Library, 1948), pp. 200–202.

15. *Lettre de Taizé,* May 1977.

16. Jean-Francis Held, *Nouvel Observateur* 625:74.

17. Obviously without excluding male homosexual families with adopted children, unmarried women with their own children, and other different and broader forms of sharing life together.

Chapter 7: The Wind Is Rising

1. Pastoral Message to the People of God by the National Conference of Brazilian Bishops, November 15, 1976.

2. Michel Bouttier, "Complexio oppositorum," *New Testament Studies* 23:18.

3. J. A. T. Robinson, *The New Reformation* (London: SCM Press, 1965), p. 16.

4. A complete report on this significant "incident" as well as the sermon of Pastor Michel Freychet can be obtained from the Reformed Church of Montpellier, 25 rue Maguelone, 34000 Montpellier, France.

5. "Actes du Synode National de Creil" (Paris: Eglise réformée de France, 1976), pp. 239 ff.

6. *Venceremos! The Speeches and Writings of Ernesto Che Guevara,* ed. John Gerassi (New York: Macmillan, 1968), p. 141.

7. Che Guevara, "El partido marxista-leninista," *Verde Olivo,* January 26, 1964.

8. Personal notes taken at the continental conference of ISAL, Oaxtepec, Mexico, 1970.

9. Mimeographed text issued by the Reformed Church, 3 rue Hoche, 78000 Versailles.

10. *Réforme* 1647.

11. *Réforme* 1659.

12. See Fernando Belo on Mark 14:17–26 in *A Materialist Reading of the Gospel of Mark* (Maryknoll, N.Y.: Orbis, 1981). The multitude not present in the upper room is included in the perspective of the many making the exodus journey.

13. The eucharist has a social and recreational aspect, a fundamentally popular character, and an unrestricted openness expressed by the host who put *no conditions* on his guests save that they accept his invitation.

That Jesus wanted *all* to come to his table is emphasized by the four evangelists, who tell us no fewer than six times that Jesus shared bread and fish with the multitude. When we realize to what degree the churches have sacralized this festive picnic, we come to understand the dynamic and prophetically subversive nature it originally had and could still have.

14. See "Un geste risqué," *Christianisme social* 7-10 (1968): some texts of a book whose publication was forbidden.

15. Wilfred Monod, *Prédication prononcée en 1900* (Paris: Berger-Levrault).

16. See Georges Casalis, "L'oecuménisme écartelé," *Notre Combat* 53 (December 1971).

17. See Michel Séguier, "Critique institutionnelle et créativité collective," INODEP working paper no. 4, Paris: l'Harmattan, 1976.

Epilogue: A Provisional Evaluation

1. Karl Marx, *Contribution to the Critique of Hegel's Philosophy of Right* in *The Marx-Engels Reader* (New York: Norton, 1972), p. 12.

2. *Christians and Socialism: Documentation of the Christians for Socialism Movement in Latin America,* ed. John Eagleson (Maryknoll, N.Y.: Orbis, 1975), pp. 174-75.

Appendix

1. See F. W. Marquardt, *Theologie und Sozialismus; Das Beispiel Karl Barths* (Berlin: Grünewald; Munich: Kaiser, 1972.

2. Throughout the research of countertheology, women's liberation, which *must* be taken into account, is an essential element in the contestation with institutional and intellectual structures of the clerical apparatus and of its ideological instruments—the dominating theology. If we have not here developed this decisive aspect of militant engagement, it is because we take seriously the advice of Sartre to men: "Keep quiet and carry the luggage." So too the advice of Benîte Groult: "There is only one way for a man to promote feminism today: to finally keep silence about feminism. Let women speak."

3. See note 2, above.

4. Jean Daniel says this very well: "I have a tendency to fight shy of the famous dictum '*everything is political,*' which is dangerous when it suggests that politics has an answer to all the sufferings of existence and holds a panacea for them. This is the kind of promise that we can no longer make to those whom we invite to struggle at our side. Do not feel that this is a sort of 'demobilization': today there are strategic bases for

every kind of struggle. But we shall not have the classless society tomorrow, and even in the classless society not all problems will be solved. We cannot yet guarantee the elimination of hereditary inequalities, or the healing of all neuroses, or, above all, the solution of the problems that have always accompanied human history—the problems of birth, suffering, and death. There is so much honest hope to give to those who suffer from oppression and alienation that I see no reason to go beyond and announce miracles—unless you want to give new life to religious fanaticism by preaching false science, thus giving new prestige to an old drug. The revolution must be considered both as indispensable and modest. The error is to believe that we have a right to everything. Nobody has promised us anything, neither God nor history. We have got to fight for something that is not Everything. When you understand that, you have reached your 'second life' " ("La deuxième vie," *Le Matin,* May 23, 1977).

    5. DIAL (Paris), no. 339, pp. 6 and 10.

Index

Compiled by William E. Jerman

Other Orbis Books . . .

CABESTRERO, Teófilo
FAITH: CONVERSATIONS WITH CONTEMPORARY THEOLOGIANS

"*Conversations* shows what an informed and perceptive journalist can do to make theology understandable, inviting and demanding. These records of taped interviews, which were compiled by Teófilo Cabestrero, a Spanish priest-journalist who lives in Paraguay, contain the opinions of fifteen well-known European and Latin American theologians (Ladislaus Boros, Georges Casalis, José Comblin, Enrique D. Dussel, Segundo Galilea, Giulio Giraldi, José María González-Ruiz, Gustavo Gutiérrez, Hans Küng, Jürgen Moltmann, Karl Rahner, Joseph Ratzinger, Edward Schillebeeckx, Juan Luis Segundo, Jean-Marie Tillard). This is perhaps why these pages are so exciting to read, even to the layman. Cabestrero ably sets up his interviews, adapting himself to the personality of each interlocutor, at times questioning, sometimes probing and at other times raising his own objections. In the end we have a thought-provoking mosaic of contemporary theological thought." *Messenger of St. Anthony*

ISBN 0-88344-126-8   *208pp. Paper $7.95*

DONDERS, Joseph G.
THE PEACE OF JESUS
*Reflections on the Gospel
for the A-Cycle*

A book of reflections based on the Sunday gospels of the A-year of the liturgical cycle. The author writes the stories of the

Gospel in colloquial and contemporary language, providing angles of insight on familiar passages and nudges toward human need on our scene.

"We listen to Joseph Donders not because he has a profound insight or handle on the son of God, but rather because Donders exalts Jesus as the center of personal life, the only positive side of reality. . . . Many a writer has attempted to describe Jesus' message of love and compassion only to find it often defies translation. In Joseph Donders' case much of that joy is communicable." *Religious Book Review*

Joseph G. Donders is author of *Jesus, the Stranger,* winner of the 1979 National Religious Book Award, *The Jesus Community,* and *The Jesus Option,* all published by Orbis.

ISBN 0-88344-379-1   *312pp. Paper $9.95*

DORR, Donal
OPTION FOR THE POOR
A Hundred Years of Vatican Social Teaching

As part of its commitment to human liberation, the Church in Latin America calls for an 'option for the poor.' Does such an option mean adopting a new direction or is it in line with the mainstream tradition of Catholic social teaching?

Donal Dorr seeks to answer this question by a careful examination of the social teaching of the Catholic Church over the past hundred years in order to find out what Church leaders have to say about poverty and social injustice. He makes a thorough and balanced study of the teaching of popes, councils and synods—and shows that the notion of an 'option for the poor' has a solid traditional basis.

Option for the Poor is an original, balanced and timely study which gets behind the prejudices of current controversy about liberation theology.

Donal Dorr is an Irish missionary priest who has done extensive academic and pastoral work in Africa and Brazil.

ISBN 0-88344-365-1   *336pp. Paper $11.95*

KAVANAUGH, John Francis
FOLLOWING CHRIST IN A CONSUMER SOCIETY
The Spirituality of
Cultural Resistance

"Father Kavanaugh succeeds in combining a sharp and uncompromising analysis of our contemporary consumer culture with gentle, compassionate and hope-filled reflection on the power of the Gospel to transform our cluttered lives. For the social activists who have lost confidence in the spiritual wellsprings of their activism, and for those who do not see the connections between their religious faith and economic and political issues, the author offers new confidence in inescapable connections. The book is a most incisive demonstration of how personal, family and community life are undermined by the prevailing values in this society. What is called for is a life of 'cultural resistance,' made possible by a new spirituality."

Alternatives

"Kavanaugh, a Jesuit, teaches philosophy at St. Louis University. The book, however, is not floating on philosophical abstractions or sinking under the weight of academic footnotes. This is, instead, a personal essay. The style is always clear, though the mood is sometimes close to rage. It is the kind of social criticism one has come to expect and appreciate from *Orbis*. It is easy reading for lower-division undergraduates."

Choice

ISBN 0-88344-090-3   *186pp. Paper $6.95*

LIBANIO, J.B.
SPIRITUAL DISCERNMENT AND POLITICS
Guidelines for Religious Communities

"Those who are really committed to relating their theology of justice to concrete socio-political options will be thankful for this book. As clear, insightful, and biblically faithful a piece of writing on hermeneutics as I have recently seen."

Alfred Krass, Editor-at-Large, The Other Side

ISBN 0-88344-463-1   *140pp. Paper $6.95*

RICHARD, Pablo *et al.*
THE IDOLS OF DEATH
AND THE GOD OF LIFE
A Theology

"There is a seismic shift taking place in the foundations of theology, and its epicenter is Latin America. Liberation theology is no fad, but a revolution in the very terms of theological work. It locates the ultimate questions not in meaning but survival; not feeling justified but in doing justice; not in belief in God but in the critique of idolatry; not in theodicy but anthropodicy; not in spiritualism but in the spirituality of the material; and most important and least understood and observed of all, not in idealist theorizing but in historical praxis. Even where their way is not our way, we need to listen to what they have learned. These essays make an excellent listening-post." *Walter Wink*

Contents: I. *Richard, Biblical Theology of Confrontation with Idols,* II. *Croatto, The Gods of Oppression,* III. *Pixley, Divine Judgment in History,* IV. *Sobrino, The Epiphany of the God of Life in Jesus Christ,* V. *Araya, The God of the Strategic Covenant,* VI. *Casañas, The Task of Making God Exist,* VII. *Limón, Meditation on the God of the Poor,* VIII. *Betto, God Bursts Forth in the Experience of Life,* IX. *Hinkelammert, The Economic Roots of Idolatry: Entrepreneurial Metaphysics,* X. *Assmann, The Faith of the Poor in Their Struggle with Idols.*

ISBN 0-88344-048-2   *240pp. Paper $12.95*

SEGUNDO, Juan Luis
THE LIBERATION OF THEOLOGY

"This is not just another title in the recent deluge of writings on liberation theology. Authored by one of the movement's primary architects, it offers both a clarifying elaboration of basic tenets and a hefty response to contemporary critics. . . . Makes for exciting reading and should not be missing in any theological library." *Library Journal*

ISBN 0-88344-285-X   *248pp. Paper $8.95*